The Awakening Handbook

30 Lessons to Manifest The Life of Your Dreams

BY

ANDY ALBERLAN

The Awakening Handbook
30 Lessons to Manifest The Life of Your Dreams

Publisher/Cover Design: Kelly Chiasson, Inspired from The Inside Out
Editor: Linsey Fischer
Proofed by: Samantha Glass
Layout: Philip Alera

ISBN: 978-1-63972-835-0

TABLE OF CONTENTS

FOREWORD

☙❧

The mid-1980s seems like a lifetime ago. Much of the memories I have from those days and years have been obscured by the passing of time. However, there are a few that stand out among the countless grains that have passed through the hourglass. One of them being the time I met the person who has become, over the vast years, my best friend. While I cannot recall the exact moment, I can recall the feelings I had.

This might come as a surprise (especially as you read on); I had an instant feeling of animosity towards Andy (Andrew). There was no reason; it was simply that he was the new kid in our small 20-25 children to a grade satellite school building. After a couple of years, the district closed the satellite school down, and all of us kids that had only known one teacher per grade were moved to the main district buildings in town.

Fast forward to the mid 1990's and life had mostly gone on without much contact between Andy and myself as we were separated by a couple of grade differences. Call it fate, call it chance, call it what you will, but I eventually became close friends with Andy's younger sister Sarah and her friends, and one day, shortly before I was to graduate high school, they invited me to come and hang out with them at the pool at Andy and

Sarah's parents' house. This was a day that even though it was 25 years ago, that I would remember for the rest of my time.

Andy came down from his private space above the little carriage barn, 'The Loft,' as it became known, and wandered over to where the rest of us were hanging out. He saw me, and the look on his face was not one that was friendly, nor was it one that was really cold or angry either, he asked what I was doing there, and I remember replying somewhat snarky, "what's it look like? Hanging out with my friends." He left, and a little while later came back, and invited me up to the loft. Hesitantly I went. It was either going to go one of two ways and I will not say which I thought it was going to go at that point.

Not much was said initially. We sat at the table in this little cramped loft space full of ancient well used furniture, rickety chairs, with posters of Iron Maiden stapled to the ceiling. After a little while, Andy brought up the past, saying: "I absolutely hated you." To which I replied, "the feeling was the same."

After a minute or two, we both came to the same conclusion, that we literally had no reason for hating each other for all of those years. It was a laughable and remarkable moment because from that time on, Andy and I have been each other's support system, learning, teaching, laughing, and propping each other up in moments of weakness, congratulating each other on our accomplishments.

The thing about getting to know someone like Andy is that he's the type of person who will call you on your bs, sometimes not so kindly, but always coming from a loving place. He's been a massively positive influence in my life over the years, watched me self-destruct, and supported me through my many successes, even when my own personal demons have sought to drag me down. If I can call one person my best friend, it is Andy.

Having been his friend for twenty-five plus years, seeing all that he's gone through in life, on a personal insider level, I can say—without a doubt—he's one of the most resilient humans I've ever had the pleasure to know. Life has thrown many curveballs his way, and while, like the rest of us, he struggles for a time, he always comes out swinging, crushing the ball out of the park to put it in a metaphorical way.

It's not just a positive attitude that separates him from the masses. It's the way he cuts through the mess, looking at the causes, dissecting his own psyche in such a way that allows him to step outside of himself to see a clear path ahead, and forging his way to successfully overcoming any obstacles placed in his way, whether placed there by others or even his own mind.

As a witness and a friend, I can speak to the steady nature Andy exhibits in his life when it comes to conquering obstacles and the impactful way he positively influences others around him, whether they are in his life for a moment or many years. Many people have come and gone throughout my time of knowing Andy, and each one of them has been impacted in a meaningful way just from having known him.

This book is just a small offering of the kindness and thoughtful care that I've known throughout the years. I know in my heart that starting out on this journey will change lives, just as it did for me all those years ago,

Brandon Blount-Carpenter

Bio: Brandon Blount- Carpenter is a naturalist, artist, and professional photographer, a loving husband that lives and thrives on his rural 145-acre property at the foothills of the Adirondack mountains, providing outdoor adventures and education to family and friends.

INTRODUCTION

❧

Today is the Day you begin manifesting the life of your dreams.

That notion might have you asking many questions. What is Manifesting? What is the life of your dreams? It is different for every one of us. Did you know that you attract what you are, not necessarily what you want in a vibrational universe? What if I told you all there is, is 'Now,' and that it takes ninety days to get the ball rolling? Have I got your attention yet?

If so, you must understand that awareness is important to begin, awareness of what, you ask? How about everything? You will learn that gratitude is essential to growth, that forgiveness is freedom, and attitude is everything. These are not just catch phrases but building blocks to creating the life of your dreams.

Stay with me. We are just getting started! There is so much to learn. Such as: the importance of listening to your intuition—you know, that guiding voice from within? Did you know that visualization is not just daydreaming anymore and that meditation comes in many forms, it's not as hard as you think?

In this book, we will discuss the life-changing shift of viewing all experiences as a blessing or a lesson. They are often both the empowering idea that happiness is a decision, not a destination and that excitement and nervousness are the same emotion viewed differently, while fear and anger are kissing cousins. Can you feel the excitement?

Together we will explore the age-old battle within, 'Love vs. Fear;' along with its neighbor, 'Success vs. Failure.' We will recognize the power within that you create when you make a decision. And hone in on the fact that if it's all about you, then you are able to flip that mindset to: everything is a win—from I can't, to I can, to I Am. We will also look at some hard truths such as, no one will believe in you, until you do and it's not really about the money.

Are you ready to be a risk-taker and follow your heart? Let it be Easy and Take Action!

Just remember, the universe loves deadlines too. So, to complete our journey; a word of caution, with great power comes great responsibility.

Are you intrigued?

Join me on a thirty-day journey, where each day we will lay the building blocks for the greatest transformation ever, Manifesting the Life of your dreams.

Today is the day!

Let's begin,

Andy Alberlan

LESSON #1

What is Manifesting?

∽

Keep your thoughts positive, they become your words.
Keep your words positive, they become your behavior.
Keep your behavior positive, they become your habits.
Keep your habits positive, they become your values.
Keep your values positive, they become your destiny.
—Mahatma Gandhi

The power of manifestation is being able to harness your true destinies in life, subconsciously put into vision, and then brought into reality. Everything you want out of the universe is already yours. The clearer your thoughts and thinking on the matter, the more timely and precise the delivery will come.

As we move through this book together, you will discover that many of my lessons are intertwined. We will study the 'why's' and practice the 'how's.' And look at all of these concepts and activities as pieces of a much larger puzzle. That is the whole of our universe, of which we only perceive and understand a fraction of.

When we discuss manifestation, it, like so many of our other topics, is one of great depth. Our purpose here is to offer an introduction, to create awareness, and inspire further exploration into these matters. This may take a lifetime, perhaps more, but what better way to spend that time? After all, this is why we are here.

In essence, manifestation is the process of bringing what exists in the mind, on the spiritual plane in the infinite intelligence or the imagination into being here and now. This is not something that we necessarily do, but allow to be done. We must understand our powers of creation. After all, we are all manifesting our lives—individually and collectively—in the now. As we will learn in chapter four, all there is, is Now. Most of us are just doing this unconsciously, without direction or guidance of said powers of creation.

Creating by default is what many of us experience in our lives. Akin to putting the car in drive and climbing into the back seat. We are moving forward, possibly doing quite a bit of damage, we may eventually reach our destination, but we are powerless to maneuver along the way.

Then there are some of us who have been taught, again unknowingly, how to use our creative faculties. Though unsure how to explain it to another, they are met with great success in many areas of their lives. Here again, an 'unconscious competent' is not able to express their strategy, nor are they in control of it

What we are aiming for is to be consciously aware of the purpose of our capabilities. We are also looking at how we can access them while knowing the signs to look for and recognizing that our creations are on their way. And after all that, we need to be ready to receive.

What is the purpose of our creative powers of manifestation? To answer this, we must each realize that we are a piece of God, of the universe, of source energy, and of the divine intelligence that surrounds us. The bible says we were made in the likeness of God. Most often, this is taken to mean that we look like God in appearance.

It seems more accurate to conceive that in a vibrational universe, where our appearance is an illusion, which we perceive through our senses. That it is not our appearance that is God like, but more our essence. We are powerful creators, once realized, our ability to tune into infinite intelligence from which all matter and information originate, a boundless field of energy, where all that is, was, and will exists as limitless potential. This is where we as individuals and collectively have emerged and likely will soon return in this infinite game of discovery.

In this grand scheme, which is more of a strategy of creation, rather than a plan with a definitive end, each of us, as pieces of God, are seeking our true nature in order for God to more fully express its infinite self, the infinite potential.

Just as there is a mind bogglingly vast array of variety in nature, with all systems living symbiotically, in the ebb and flow of creation. So are we, pieces of the divine, expressing ourselves, our dreams, our desires for the continual expansion of this infinite creation.

When we become in tune with our truest selves, that innermost spirit and seek to manifest our dreams from the aether into existence, this is when we are closest to God.

To manifest our dreams into our reality is our purpose, here and now. There is no right. There is no wrong. There just 'is.' When you participate in this notion fully, you contribute to the collective in a way that few of us will be able to fully comprehend.

The world we live in and the reality we see before us is a collective creation of our unconscious desires—our misdirection of that power. Let us create a world that collectively serves our highest good along with the good of all the beneficiaries of our existence. Imagine the world we can create together.

How can we access our creative faculties?

The creative process is different for everyone. Just as we are all unique, so are the techniques we use to access and direct our creative power. The steps are simple, so customization is easy and encouraged. To engage the process, we must ask. That's it.

Wait. What? All I have to do is ask, that's easy enough. Isn't it? Yes, it is. But we must remember that we live in a vibrational universe. I know I mentioned this before, we will explain it more in-depth in lesson three. For now, just realize that the vibrational signal you send out, is what you receive back.

So, pleading with the universe that you desperately need something is always met with agreement. That will get you more circumstances, people, and things to match your signal. We do get what we ask for, so we must be clear and careful with our requests. Asking should be as if we are putting in a request with the universe for the materials and circumstances we require to achieve the intended goal and/or dream.

Like any good distributor or supplier, the Universe will deliver to us just what we ordered. So, it is our responsibility to make sure that order is clear, remains clear, and is properly received.

Consider this, you are building a house. You have laid the foundation and it is time to begin framing. You have a blueprint in front of you, professionally designed, stamped, ready to roll. You know exactly how this house is going to look, every piece of it. You call the local lumber yard with your order. Very precisely, you tell them all the items and quantities you require. Then after you hang up, you remember that you need it on Tuesday, not Monday, you call and reschedule.

Then you are reviewing the blueprint and you see the potential for a second bathroom, which wasn't in the original order, so you call and ask for a change order. But you talk to a different clerk. He is unaware of your first order and its complexities. Then you get a call from the client, who wants to know if a second story is possible. You call to order additional materials and cancel the order for a second bathroom because it is outside of the budget now, and you ask for it to be delivered on Thursday. Confused? Exactly.

So, when we are placing our order with the universe unconsciously, this is how we tend to do it, and we are so surprised when our order doesn't show up on time or isn't what we expected.

To place an accurate order, to make a proper request, we must be firm and clear with what we want, and when we want it, then we must not deviate from our order. To ask, we can write it, by making a list, in the present tense: "Now I am manifesting the life of my dreams!" Say it to yourself, be careful about saying it to others, after all, it's not their manifestation. Don't give them the power to discourage you, especially in the early stages. You wouldn't let a stranger hold your baby, would you? Treat this the same way, protect it, nurture it, love it, until it's ready to walk on its own.

You've got to feel it, as if it's already here. See that new car out in the driveway, feel the excitement. Live it, go see that new car, test drive it, bring home the brochures, and put them on your wall. Know it. Have a knowing that it's on its way, just like you know the Sun will rise in the morning, never doubt or deviate, just as you would never doubt that nighttime is followed by day. Just remember that the dawn comes, even if it is obscured by clouds. Believe it and you will see it.

After we have placed our clear order and know it is on its way, we must be patient during the gestation period. Like a seed that is planted in the soil, so has our seed of desire been planted in 'the universal intelligence.'

Just as a farmer does, we must be patient and care for our seed as it transforms into something tangible. Repetition of our order, gratitude for it already being here, and preparing to receive are how we bide our time.

We must not be the inexperienced farmer that plants the seed, waters it, and comes back the next day, stomping on the earth, demanding his crop. Nor should we be the farmer that nurtures his seed, watering it, fertilizing it, tending it until it sprouts, then picks the succulent baby leaves in an attempt to make a salad. We must be patient, vigilant, wise farmers that understand the cycle. 'There is a time to till. There is a time to sow. There is a time to rest. And there is a time to reap.'

With practice and patience, we can become great farmers, experienced predictors of these gestation periods. We can gauge appropriately when to sow, then get ready for the sunshine because we will be confidently aware that a quality harvest is just around the bend.

Then comes the fateful day, you have done all the leg work, the head work, the knowing, and here comes your dream. Are you ready to receive it?

Many of us drop the ball right when it is coming to us. As Abraham Hicks states emphatically, "we must be ready to be ready to be ready." We must be grateful for what we are about to receive as well as willing and able to receive it in the form that the universe has deemed most beneficial for our experience, which may be different than anticipated.

We cannot know all the aspects of the universe. We must then trust that all is working for our highest good. This is the basic essence of manifesting the life of your dreams. I am so happy and grateful now that you are manifesting the life of your dreams.

LESSON #2

What is The Life of Your Dreams?

❦

**This may sound like a silly question,
but what is the life of your dreams?**

Have you ever really considered it in any depth? I am willing to bet that many people have not, and of those that have, I would imagine many of those folks told themselves it wasn't possible. Do you find that to be true for you?

I know that there was a point in my life when I would have answered, Yes, to that question. Even though my life, from the outside, appeared to have all the necessary elements of a 'happy, fulfilled life.'

Inside I was struggling, drowning, gasping for breath. My spirit, my soul, always felt as if something was missing or that I was running out of time. It was a horrible feeling. And when I searched outside of myself to try and find the cause, I came up empty handed. It was very frustrating, indeed. If I would try to get more 'stuff' accomplished, to make up for the feeling that I was running out of time, then the clock would race me. Time would seem to pass faster! Have you experienced similar feelings?

What I had failed to realize in those years is that the external things in my life were not the issue, that getting more accomplished never assuaged that feeling of lack. Acquiring more stuff didn't fill the emptiness I felt. One cannot expect to put a fresh paint job on a car with a blown motor and hope that it will start, just as external solutions will not resolve internal problems.

Looking back in my life to find either the solution or to figure out where I had gone off track led me nowhere. Though, isn't that what we usually do? I think it's because we are taught as children, if we get lost, to go back and retrace our steps. Which makes sense if you have taken a wrong turn in the park and find yourself in unfamiliar territory, but in real life, it just isn't that simple because you can never go back, really. Nor should you. Looking back will never get you where you want to go.

Just as trying to drive to the store while looking in the rearview mirror is a very ineffective way to reach your destination. Looking back in your life to move forward towards the life of your dreams doesn't get you very far.

So, Let's get back to the life of your dreams. It is different for everyone. What's important is to accept where you are and to focus your attention on the future. It is okay to acknowledge the past; it served you well. As we will discover in lesson four, it is very important to bring ourselves into the present moment, as that is where clarity resides. We must focus on the future and make a plan for the life of our dreams.

This exercise we are about to do is a powerful one. I was introduced to it as part of the PGI coaching program with Bob Proctor and Cathy Gallagher. I had never before sat down and hashed things out like this. The exercise is simple, sit down and visualize your dream life in three to five years from now. Make it what you really want, not what you think your spouse wants, or your parents or your children or your neighbor or your best friend.

Write it out as you feel, deep down in your heart, every detail, again, not what you think you can get, what you WANT! Have fun, plan big, dream big, luxuriate in every detail, take your time and enjoy every minute of it. Put how much money you want to make and an ideal method for its acquisition.

Write this out in a present tense, make it as long or short as you please, but don't leave anything out. It might even feel a little scary. Your brain might even tense up. You may feel chills or butterflies in your stomach. For many, this may be the first time they are honest with themselves about what they truly want; that can be a little unsettling.

Just get started by saying: "I see my life projected out 3-5 years and I am so happy and grateful now that...." and let it flow. No harm in dreaming, and this is your dream, so make it a good one. Make it a dream that gets you feeling giddy inside, makes your body tingle. A dream that you want to read over and over again because it is so delicious.

Once you have done this and are satisfied, read it over a few times and put it away. No need to share it with anyone unless you really trust them. Read your dream periodically, or better yet, everyday. Early morning, perhaps with your coffee or just before bed, is the best time to read over your dream. Feel free to make additions and adjustments to your dream, whatever feels right. You can write out several different dreams and see which one you like best.

Just remember, you are a powerful creator. When you fall in love with your dream, you are bringing it on its way. So, start getting ready to receive as the life of your dreams has already begun to take shape beyond your awareness. It is going to be amazing. I am so happy and grateful now that the life of your dreams has arrived.

LESSON #3

You attract what you are..

(NOT NECESSARILY WHAT YOU WANT)

⚮

*"You don't attract what you want, you attract what you are.
Take responsibility for everything that's showing up in your life
because it's reflecting back to you.
Who you believe yourself to be and
what you believe is possible."*
—Anastasia Netri

All that we are able to perceive in this world around us and the known universe, both on the macroscopic and microscopic levels, is in motion.

"We are living in an ocean of motion" as Bob Proctor puts it, and Einstein stated, "Nothing happens until something moves. When something vibrates, the electrons of the entire universe resonate with it."

Great minds hinting towards the active state of all matter is vibration. Much like the strings of a guitar, which vibrate both as waves and particles. Observed at a quantum level should vibrate as individual units of energy known as phonons. When the guitar strings vibrate, a sound is emitted in our reality. These vibrations can be tuned up or down to match similar frequencies. When two notes are played together, they are known to harmonize.

Much like the strings of a guitar, we can adjust our frequency and tune up to higher or lower vibration. When we interact as two notes together, we can either harmonize with that frequency or become dissonant, where our vibrations do not match. Typically, we will attract that which we harmonize with.

We live in a vibrational reality. Vibration in quantum physics means that everything is energy. Each vibration is equivalent to a feeling and in the vibrational world. There are only two types of vibration: positive and negative. Any feeling that causes you to emit a vibration is seen as positive or negative. Much like the poles of a magnet, which either attract each other or repel each other. So are we, on a vibrational level.

Science seeks to understand: 'what is the world?' while spirituality seeks to discover 'who or what is man?' Intelligence is knowing others, and wisdom is knowing self. Our modern society has been obsessed with understanding and mastering the outside world. Over the past few decades, a growing movement to understand the inner world has unfolded. The blending of science and spirituality is nothing new, indeed, they are siblings, meant to walk hand in hand.

Harmony, frequency, vibration, and attraction are both spiritual in nature as well as scientific. There is a significant overlap between the two. More and more, the Law of Attraction is considered a key concept to shaping our reality. The complexities of quantum physics and the effects that our thoughts and observations have on the elemental levels of our known reality are beyond our scope here, but one can certainly begin to see evidence of this in what is known as the double-slit experiment, which demonstrates that light and matter can change its form and behavior depending on the observer. It is certainly a fascinating subject and one that can be challenging to explain by science alone.

We cannot even begin to discuss the Law of Attraction without mentioning Rhonda Byrne's 2006 film: 'The Secret.' It is undoubtedly a starting place for millions of people as the first time they were introduced to the power of attraction and the effect it can have on our lives. It is also a great jumpstart into learning some of the world's most renowned teachers on the subject. Bob Proctor, Lisa Nichols, Joe Vitale, Jack Canfield to name a few, the list goes on. Each of these teachers brings to the table a lifetime of knowledge and experience, delivering the message of attraction in their own unique ways.

Simply put, the Law of Attraction states that positive or negative thoughts bring positive or negative experiences into a person's life. This Simplicity makes the Law of Attraction, well, seemingly attractive, but there is more to it. The law of attraction is a secondary law. The primary law is the law of vibration, which states that everything is energy and that energy is vibrating at a certain frequency. Nothing is at rest.

Now that we have some awareness of these two fundamental laws and how they interact with each other, let's attempt to put them into simple to understand terms and see how they can play out in our reality.

As previously mentioned, we are vibrational beings in a vibrational reality. Our brains and our senses interpret these vibrations and we perceive the physical illusion that we agree is 'reality.' We, as vibrational beings, are much like the guitar strings. We can be tuned to raise or lower our frequency by the thoughts we think and emotions we feel. Thoughts are energy forms that are not originating in the brain, but are 'picked up' by the brain. Imagine that the brain is like a switching station, sending and receiving transmissions and turning them into thought-forms. If this is the case, that begs the question: If we do not think thoughts, where do they originate?

Thoughts originate in the mind, but the mind is not the brain. The brain is the receiving organ of the mind, which is outside the body. Think of satellites floating in space, transmitting data from space to earth. This is very much how thoughts function.

When you listen to the radio, you are using a device very similar to the brain. By adjusting the frequency setting on the dial, you are able to tune in to that frequency and access the information being broadcast on that signal. If you are looking for country music to play on your radio and the frequency for that station is 100.7 hertz, then you will not be able to access the information you are looking for by tuning into 96.8 hertz. We, as humans, function on a thought level, similar to this.

Higher frequency vibration is considered positive, and lower frequency vibration is considered negative. Typically on an emotional frequency chart, in which many variations can be found online, 200 hertz categorized as the frequency of courage and lower are considered negative.

Frequencies of 200 hertz and higher are considered positive. For instance, the lowest measurable frequency is 20 hertz, which is 'shame;' how many of us have experienced that low-level vibration? It does not feel good, lowest of the low, indeed. Alternatively, at 528 hertz, we find love. Incidentally, this is not the highest level of vibration, which is enlightenment at 700 hertz. That high level vibration is only obtained through years of dedicated mastery of self, this is the arena of Jesus, Buddha, Allah and the like. For the rest of us, Love is a very high vibrational frequency, one that we have all experienced at one time or another.

A greater understanding of the vibrational frequency and emotions can be obtained through the book: *Power vs. Force* by David R Hawkins MD; PhD, a widely known authority in the fields of consciousness research and spirituality. This is initially where the emotional frequency chart was established. The basic premise: if we harmonize in thought to lower levels of vibration and stay there, then we are only open to receive those experiences which match our level of vibration.

The opposite is also true. If we seek to raise our level of vibration to increasingly higher frequencies, then we will harmonize with the information and experiences that exist at those levels, and lower-level experiences will fall away. Indeed a fascinating subject and well worth further exploration.

Whereas Dr. Hawkins trended more on the scientific side of our aforementioned siblings. On our spiritual side, we have Abraham Hicks, who is perhaps one of the best-known teachers of the Law of Attraction. A multitude of videos can be found online and several books have been published over the course of thirty years, including: *The Law of Attraction*, *Ask and it is Given*, and *The Vortex.*

Abraham Hicks, who is actually a woman named Esther Hicks, is channeling source energy called Abraham. This may sound like a bit of a fishy concept at first. I think that Esther certainly thought it was in the early days, but once you come to accept it for what it is, the information and the delivery are quite delightful. The message is delivered in a thousand different ways using humorous anecdotes about Esther's travels and day-to-day experiences to illustrate the same basic premise. Source energy wants you to know and understand that all you could ever imagine is waiting for you in a vibrational escrow, a universal bank account of sorts, called the Vortex.

When you harmonize with this Vortex of creation, then that which is in your Vortex, is a culmination of your earthly and spiritual desires. Everything you have ever dreamed, imagined, or asked for is brought ever closer to you and begins to manifest in your life. There is nothing quite like starting your day with a rampage of attraction. Learning how to raise your vibration with a rampage is both fun and will leave you elevated, light and hopeful. Check it out.

Another example of how our emotional frequency translates into our reality can be found through the studies of Masaru Emoto. Mr. Emoto, is an internationally renowned Japanese researcher who has been able to capture the structure of water at the moment of freezing on film under a microscope. His books: *The Miracle of Water* and *The Hidden Messages in Water* are eye opening to say the least.

Mr Emoto's experiments were simple, he would write emotional word messages onto beakers of water or play music, this subjected the water to the vibrational frequency of the emotions or music, then he photographed the structure of the water at the time of freezing under a microscope. The results are truly astounding.

The water subjected to low vibration emotion ie; anger, fear, hate, was structurally lopsided and distorted, often the structures were 'ill' looking and damaged. The water that was subjected to positive vibration emotions ie; love, kindness, friendship, were structurally symmetrical and vibrantly beautiful. The implications of this type of study are truly thought provoking in that the human body is made up of approx. 70 percent water, similarly our earth is also 70 percent water, coincidence? I think not.

Even so, Mr. Emoto's experiments cause us to consider the ramifications of our collective thoughts and actions concerning ourselves and our planet. Perhaps the sacredness of water, the essential giver of life, has been abandoned as a concept for too long. Considering the industrial uses of water and the fact that we abuse water and treating its seemingly miraculous properties with such poor regard. It would account for a lot of what we see in our personal and collective levels of health and well being, as well as that of the planet as a whole.

There have been other numerous studies about plants also reacting to emotions. I would extend this to animals as well, we can all tell the difference between a dog that is beaten and abused and one that is nurtured, pampered and loved.

When we open our eyes and minds, the evidence is all around us, our thoughts and emotions are powerful. We are the creators of our experience, individually and collectively. We attract on a vibrational level, not what we want, but what harmonizes with us at a level of frequency. The mass of the human population of earth vibrates at 200 hertz or lower, anger, fear, grief, guilt, and shame. We can see the effect of this on the current state of our world.

Just imagine for a moment if each and every one of us, 7.7 billion souls and counting, could raise our vibration to the frequency of love, 528 hertz, and hold it there, collectively, unanimously, simultaneously for just five minutes. Just imagine the world we could create together then. I pray for that day, join me, and we will bring it ever closer as we manifest the life of our dreams. Thank you.

LESSON #4

Today is Only Yesterday's Tomorrow

∽

*"People don't realize that now is all there is.
There is no past or future except as memory or
anticipation in your mind."*
—Eckhart Tolle

In our society, in this day and age, we lead busy lives. Are we not taught to be this way? When we were children, we were asked, what do we want to be when we grow up? When we were in grade school, we were encouraged to think about our future careers. In high school, we were asked to consider what we will do next. College? Military? Vocational School?

Once we are in the workforce, we are working towards advancement, higher pay, better office, bigger title, and of course the old stick and carrot, retirement. How many people have held their sights firmly on that target for 20-30 years? Enduring all manner of heartache and misery, only to reach retirement and find it to be unfulfilling. Many people who have strived their whole lives wind up in decline at retirement with prolonged occurrence of disease or death that follow all too soon.

What is the purpose of this perpetual striving in our society? Have you ever taken a moment to wonder, "Why the hell am I doing this?"

Trading my current time, energy, mental capacity, blood, sweat and tears for some future payout. If you are among those that have considered this question, congratulations, that is likely why you are reading this book. For every one of us that is willing to contemplate that question and seek out answers; there are countless more that never bother to pay attention or are unable to handle the fact that what they are doing with their life may not necessarily be in their best interest.

The fact is that tomorrow is not guaranteed and yesterday is no longer here. The title of this lesson is from a song that I remember from my childhood, A British rock band from the 70s, Uriah Heep. The song is called Circle of Hands; the lyric that has rung in my ears for so many years, "today is only yesterday's tomorrow" has had me thinking about how important being here now is. Wise words indeed, for all we ever really have to work with is now.

Our lives, even as we are taught to see them as a linear series of events, occasions, or milestones, measured in trips around the sun which we call years, are nothing more than endless moments of now. One might agree that those 'nows' will end at the time of our death, but we do not definitively know that those Nows, that perpetual state of in the moment, does not continue for the soul as it journeys to other worldly realms.

For our purposes, we will stick to the concept of our lives being a perpetual series of moments that we will call 'Now.' When can you take action? Only in the Now. You cannot take action yesterday, or a year from Now; those do not exist. Similarly, we have a choice; we can choose how we feel about the Now. Will we embrace the sacred nature of the Now? Revel in it? Appreciate it for what it is? And love ourselves and our lives in the Now? Or will we see our Now as drudgery, misery, pain, hardship, or something similar to mental or emotional torture that we must endure to get to some future existence where relief and hopefully happiness will meet us?

How many of us have found ourselves in the latter situation? Working a job or enduring a family life that did not serve us or drained the life force from us, to the point where all we did was daydream about some distant future where it would all be better, while cursing our present moment? I am sure a great many people can relate, I know that I can. Sad really, when you think about it. To waste so many potentially beautiful moments that will never present themselves again.

So, what can we do about it? How can we live more fully in the Now and embrace it in a way that there are no more wasted moments in our lives?

Once we acknowledge the reality that our lives are lived in the Now, we are more fully able to consider how we are going to spend those fleeting moments. We can begin to cherish each one as the precious gift that it is, to be in awe of the fullness of the moment. Often it can be difficult to do this, living our lives at the breakneck speed that we do. This is akin to trying to get a good look at an object laying on the side of the highway when we are in a vehicle traveling 75-80 mph; it tends to be an indistinguishable blur.

We really have only lived our lives at this speed for the past century. Before that, most people's lives moved at the pace of a trotting horse, so this is certainly an unnatural pace, it's no wonder it has become a cause of so much stress and anxiety for us.

In order to really capture the moment and appreciate it for what it is, we must slow down. It is only when we throttle back and consciously choose to revel in the moment that we can see what we may have been missing all along.

It is a common phrase among parents at their children's high school graduation. They look at their child, all grown up, ready to take on the world. You hear them say, "My baby, all grown up, where did the time go?" A puzzling statement to say the least. One must speculate that the parents were there. I mean someone had to raise that young man or lady. Right? Do the parents have amnesia about what has happened over the past eighteen years? Likely not.

This is the perfect example of the way we view our lives, not in the Now. A parent raising a child, or children is often buried in activity, running low on sleep, pulled in multiple directions at once. Many are keeping their sights set on the day the baby will be born, when the baby is potty trained, when the child starts kindergarten so mom can have a break, when will they hit puberty, when will they make the football team, what college will they go to and BOOM. Eighteen years have passed, always looking forward to the next milestone, now they are looking back at the blur, wondering what happened. Why?

Because we are not taught to cherish each moment, often it takes a crisis, a health scare, the threat of loss of a loved one or a near death experience for us to value those moments and to live fully in the Now. After all, that's all there is.

As stated previously, the purpose of this book is to be an introduction to these thought provoking concepts. Not to be an in depth study of each subject. Many of these ideas are profoundly deep, with a great deal of information on them, presented by teachers that have dedicated an incredible amount of time and effort, often years, researching and writing about them.

One such teacher, especially on this subject, who is quoted in the opening of this lesson is Eckhart Tolle. In his book: *The Power of Now*, he takes an in-depth look at the benefits of being present and the role that the ego plays with regard to our ability to stay present. There are also many videos and interviews exploring 'The Now' online with Eckhart. He is an interesting and insightful individual, to say the least.

To be more present, what we must do, and this is something that must be practiced if it is a new concept, is get out of our head. We must detach from the running monologue of thoughts that play out as to-do lists, minute by minute scheduling hurdles and deadlines, problem/ reaction scenarios, and internal conflict arguments.

To detach from that level of thought, Now, we have to step outside the mind. To step outside the mind, we must focus on our breath, taking three conscious breaths where we inhale for a six count, hold it for a six count and exhale in a six count. This relaxes the brain and the body; helping us to be more present in the moment.

As a matter of practice, step outside, inhale deeply, note the smell of the air, feel the air temperature on your skin, do not judge, just feel it. Acknowledge the dew on the grass, see how it sparkles in the morning sun, listen to the rustle of leaves on the breeze, be aware of all the individual edges sliding together to make that sound. Feel the breeze, close your eyes and turn to face the direction of the wind, listen to the birds sing, hear their interplay as they call to each other, their song today is for you and you only. Pause and acknowledge the color of the sky, see the clouds as they drift and change, realize that those clouds only exist Now, for you, consider that they will never appear quite the same again.

Reach out and touch the bark of a tree, feel its texture and imagine all that it took to create such a thing, for you to experience. Now, run your fingers over the smooth paint job on your car and feel its silkiness as it flows under your fingertips, contemplate all that needs to occur for you to move your hand while touching that car, moving perfectly, functioning in concert in one fluid movement without effort.

This is living in the present moment, detached from the overworked mind. With practice, you can spend more and more time in conscious awareness of the world around you, and with practice, will more fully be able to embrace the Now. Once we are aware of and able to embrace the Now and all it's precious, fleeting moments, we can more fully appreciate the life of our dreams we have manifested, here and Now.

LESSON #5

It Takes 90 Days To Get The Ball Rolling

❦

Have you ever tried to create a new healthy habit or make a different lifestyle choice? We have all encountered the daunting task of starting a new habit, or breaking away from a bad one. The sad truth is that for most of us, creating a bad habit only requires it to be done several times and it is already becoming ingrained into our lives.

This is likely due to the fact that these bad habits, whatever they may be, smoking, eating sweets or fatty, greasy foods, binge-watching an interesting show, the list goes on, are serving or fulfilling some sort of need or desire that resides within our subconscious mind. This hidden need or desire is in the background, below our radar, directing our behavior to its own ends.

For instance, perhaps you, like me, grew up in a family that smoked cigarettes. Now, at the time, the late 70's and early 80's, of my childhood, this was completely normal. What we must take a moment to understand is that the first seven years of life, from conception to the age of about seven, we are in an unconscious state called the Theta state. This dream-like state is what makes children act like children.

It is the brain wave state where we are most susceptible to suggestion, this is the state where a hypnotist is able to influence behavior through the power of suggestion. This is the time of life and the brain wave state where our subconscious minds are programmed to traverse and gain the intricate knowledge needed to live in our culture, to understand societal and social norms, to become a mirror image of those around us so that we will fit in.

At the time of my childhood, smoking was a prevalent habit in our society, everybody smoked or it seemed that way. People smoked in restaurants, in their cars, at work, in airports and even on airplanes themselves, if one can imagine that in this day and age. It was just something that pretty much everyone did, especially in their homes. I like so many of my generation who literally grew up immersed in a cloud of cigarette smoke.

My subconscious mind, the one being programmed in those first seven years, the one that instilled societal norms, that was programmed to differentiate between what was safe and what wasn't, what constituted nurturing, safety, love, was programmed that cigarettes and the smell associated with them, was good. It was programmed that the activity surrounding smoking cigarettes was not only cool and desirable, but it equated home, security, love, protection and friendship. This became ingrained deep into my subconscious mind, as I am quite sure it did for so many of my peers.

Fast forward to the relative age of puberty and the desire began to fester in me, to be like those around me and play out my program. Just as a computer must run the software that it is programmed with, so are we. I was told not to smoke, by my parents, by their friends, by my teachers. I was instructed and educated as to the health risks of smoking at school, by television commercial campaigns and billboards.

I was told "Smoking causes lung cancer and death." Heck, it says it right on the pack. It didn't matter. It was programmed into me, into my subconscious mind, which was running behind the scenes, beyond my awareness, night and day. Their messages were directed at my conscious mind, to which all they had to say made perfect sense.

One day around the 7th grade, I got a hold of some cigarettes. I lit one up, since that's what you did with cigarettes. It was horrible, I coughed and coughed. Once I caught my breath, I took another drag, coughed a little, but not so much, this time it wasn't so bad. I found that if I just took it easy, I could handle it. My mouth felt funny and I had to go inside and brush my teeth, but I had done it, I was on my way.

Fast forward a few weeks and a new friend asked me to come over to his house after school. He asked if I could get some cigarettes, I knew I could. The next day after school, we walked down the railroad tracks that ran through town and lit up those cigarettes. It went much better that time and I actually enjoyed it. It felt really good, as well as cool as hell, after all, it was a grown up thing to do, it felt safe and comfortable, this was part of friendship.

I was hooked, it would take me the better part of 25 years and countless attempts to detach from that habit. It was the immense love for my children and my desire to not pass this habit along to the next generation which gave me the strength and conviction to finally quit for good. It was not easy.

I feel compelled to tell you this story as it illustrates how and why bad habits can come so easily. We all have our subconscious triggers from youth, perhaps your favorite grandparent always brought you chocolate, so you associate sweets with love and acceptance.

Now as an adult, you find that you over indulge in sweets when under stress or feeling lonely. Perhaps there was no greater time in your life than clothes shopping with your mother, it was a time you spent together, got her undivided attention and were able to come home with some great new clothes that were all yours, clothes your mom told you looked great on you. Now, in your adult life, whenever you are feeling down or in need of validation, you find yourself at the mall, over spending on things that bring you that same feeling, even if it squeezes your budget.

We all have these deeply ingrained issues that can make bad habits come more easily and cause them to be very challenging to deviate from, even if we can very clearly see that they are detrimental to us in some way.

Now that we have some idea of why bad habits seem to come so easily and are difficult to break, as with so many of our other lessons, this rabbit hole of the subconscious/ conscious mind and the interplay they have in our lives is something that can be explored more deeply than we have time or space for here.

The information that is currently out there is astonishing and new information seems to be surfacing at an impressive rate. As Science and associated communities start to connect the dots as to how these two minds are tied to much of what we humans do and experience. Dr Bruce Lipton has written several books that can further explain how the subconscious mind along with our genetics control so much of our lives, *The Honeymoon Effect* and the *Biology of Belief* are a great place to start.

When it comes to creating new beneficial habits, it is not always easy or simple. Sure, many of us can get good and fired-up by saying something like, "I am going to change my diet, no more sugar or grains. From now on it's strictly broccoli, chicken and rice until I lose 35 pounds, it worked for so and so!" You think to yourself, this is gonna be great, this is my heart's desire, I can't wait.

Two days later, you swing into a gas station to pick up a package of HoHo's and a Mountain Dew, because you were so depressed about the broccoli for lunch and you not getting a piece of cake at your friends birthday party next weekend and then you were sitting at work and you heard an icecream truck go by or you thought you did, I suppose it could have just been a text message coming through in the next cubicle. Whew!

"Well, whatever. That was never going to work anyways. Gosh, this HoHo is so damn good, what was I thinking trying to give up something so delicious." So there you are, sitting in your car, not even 48 hours after you started your health kick, you are sitting there in shame, with chocolate in the corners of your mouth and an empty wrapper on your passenger seat that represents your soul.

A little dramatic, I get that. We have all been there, in our own unique ways. That's OK. What we are looking for now, to help manifest the life of our dreams, is some tangible ways, some workable information about how we can develop healthy habits and create a new lifestyle for ourselves to support our journey towards that dream.

There is a myth that it takes 21 days to form a new habit and perhaps there is some truth to that, especially with regard to younger folks. However, It has been found that as you age, it becomes more challenging to form new habits and have them stick. This is due to the existing neural pathways in the brain being deeply established. Neural pathways are like the roads of your brain, through repetition some roads are followed more frequently. Now, let's not think of those roads as a paved highway, more like a cattle trail or a deer path in the woods.

The reason we want to think of them as a cowpath or a deer trail is that each time our neurons follow a particular route, the pathway deepens, much the same as the habitual use of a trail by cattle or deer as they move along a particular route. Just as it would be challenging for a line of cattle that have followed the same well worn trail through the gate for months or years, carving a deep groove in the soil, to deviate from this trail and find itself in unfamiliar territory. So are the neural pathways of our brains, following the path of least resistance and staying in familiar territory.

There is hope, thanks to something called Neuroplasticity, also known as brain plasticity. The ability of the brain to change continuously throughout a person's life. The brain and its neural pathways are ever changing, creating new ones and discarding old unused ones.

The old-age saying, "You can't teach an old dog new tricks" is just not true. As we grow older, it can be slower and more challenging to change old habits and adopt new ways of thinking as that flexibility in the brain diminishes to some extent. This is mainly due to the fact that our habitual neural pathways are well established unlike during our developmental stages, when very few were deeply established and we were learning and changing rapidly.

Now that we have a rudimentary understanding of how the brain works, let's get back to our 21 days to form a new habit. Three weeks is a good starting point and if you can do something consistently for three weeks straight, you are well on your way, but if you really want to make that new habit into a lifestyle, on average you will need to perform it each day, without fail for 66 days.

Now, this is on average, if you are older, say in your 40's, 50's, 60's, it can take anywhere from 90 days to a year to fully form that habit so that it is ingrained into the subconscious mind.

If that sounds a bit scary or daunting, just remember that it feels really good to implement new beneficial habits. Besides, you are going to be one year older a year from now whether you form that new habit or not. So, give it a shot. If you can get to the three week mark, then extending it 90 days doesn't seem that bad, that's only 69 more days. If you extend the 90 days from the 21 you have already achieved, that's 111 days you have sustained your new habit. Nearly 1/3 of a year.

Since you were working towards creating this new habit as part of a beneficial lifestyle change, having one third of a year under your belt just feels good and you should be feeling and seeing the benefits of that change without question at that point. It can make you look forward to the next 90 days and the next 90 and the next thing you know, you will not be able to remember a time when you didn't live this way.

So, 21 days is a great start but for the vast majority of us, 90 days is the minimum amount of time it will take to form new, deep set pathways. It is also important to note that there tends to be a bump in the road of sorts at the 30 and 60 day marks, thanks again to our subconscious mind, that by then has caught wind that we are hell bent on stepping outside the established safety zone. This can come in the form of an illness, with physical symptoms such as headache, upset stomach etc., so watch out and stay aware of yourself and your condition at those milestones. You CAN reach your goal, no matter what.

One of the best ways to help ensure that you do make it through those tough times is to have an accountability partner. This is how groups such as Alcoholics Anonymous are so successful, and alcohol is not exactly an easy habit to kick, so the proof is in the pudding, as they say. To establish accountability, it must be with someone you respect and trust. This respect and trust must also be reciprocated. You are to each hold the other accountable for their actions. Make a pact, put it into writing, sign it with the desires clearly stated so that there is no gray area or discrepancy. Each day you should be in contact with your accountability partner, sharing your struggles and triumphs.

No one wants to disappoint someone they respect. This is what gives coaches and mentors so much sway, this is also how they can bring the best out of another. When you have a moment of weakness, you will think about having to disclose your temporary failure to your partner. Often, this is all the incentive you need to push through to a place of strength and overcome the urge to go back.

The subconscious mind is powerful but we as conscious, aware individuals are more powerful. As awareness increases and you gain stability within yourself, coupled with the support of like minded individuals, before long you will find yourself far along the new pathway that leads to the life of your dreams!

LESSON #6

Awareness is The Key

❧

"What is necessary to change a person is to change his awareness of himself."
—Abraham Maslow

What is the difference between a human being and a dog, besides the obvious physical differences? The level of consciousness is the biggest difference between humans and their best friends and one of the reasons we don't have to worry about dogs taking over the world.

It sounds silly but have you ever wondered why dogs don't advance in the world? They are in close contact with us, have access to all of our technology, can observe our ways and strategies, yet they are happy where they are. It's the level of awareness that keeps them where they are. Dogs are consciously aware that they are in the room, that's as far as it goes, no need to question that.

Humans are consciously aware that we are not only in the room but that we are aware that we are aware that we are in the room. Do you need to read that again, because it's true, and it leads to a lot of questions, does it not? Who am I, why am I here in this room, how did I get here and where did this room come from?

It's this level of thinking that literally sets us apart from the beasts. Awareness is how we grow, how we problem solve and a key factor to how we view ourselves and the world around us.

For instance, very few of us would set our minds to work and come up with a solution without first knowing there was a problem, would we?

Hence, this is one reason that awareness is the key to growth. By Identifying that there is an area of concern or something that can be improved upon, we begin to seek out information or solutions. This is the beginning of growth when we become aware that it is 'Us' that could use improvement.

Self-awareness, which is the trickiest thing to develop, is a paradox of sorts. It is paradoxical because to become self aware, you have to be aware enough about yourself to realize that you need to know yourself better.

Low self-awareness has been linked to poor leadership performance as well as poor mental well being and self-destructive habits along with addiction.

When you become self-aware, you become more aware of the self in others and are more able to look inside that self to see what 'makes them tick.'

To explore your own thoughts and actions, while taking responsibility for those thoughts and actions, makes you more able to understand others point of view or see the potential driving force behind their actions. While this does not justify those actions, it can certainly help to bring understanding and empathy on your part for another, which can temper your reaction and garner a meaningful response.

While there is practical awareness of your environment and awareness of self, becoming more aware of your thoughts and inner workings, there is also spiritual awareness. Spiritual awareness is a process by which we begin to explore our own being in order to become whole and reunite our spirits with our physical bodies in a commonality of purpose. We most often do this by examining our beliefs, being conscious about our intentions on any given matter.

We can expand our mind using meditation or exploring new ideas and beliefs. We may make our personal well being a priority in our lives above all else and feel a need to let go of people, places and things that no longer serve our higher good or life's intention. This letting go process can often be the most difficult at first, due to the upheaval it can cause with family, friends, spouses and children. It may come to pass that the profession you have worked in for a long time is no longer serving you on the level it once did. It can be quite the process to come to terms with the things in your life that need to be let go, but in the end those things in our life that are hardest to let go tend to be the most transformative.

Often, self-awareness and spiritual awareness go hand in hand as they are intertwined, both dealing with aspects of the inner self.

The concept of awareness on these levels can be illustrated by imagining that you are standing in a glass elevator that is located on the outside of a tall building, before you is a lush park with many trees and bushes along winding paths.

On the ground level, your awareness is of the bushes in front of you, 10-20 feet in every direction, you can see the entrance to the winding paths, but no further. You reach over and press the 'up' arrow. The elevator slowly rises, as you begin to ascend, you are able to see more of the winding paths that were previously hidden from view and see people walking along them, over the bushes and through the tree branches.

Slowly the elevator rises, now you are able to look over the tops of the trees and see the skyline in the distance. The sun becomes brighter as you rise, you can now see for miles over the treetops, there are other buildings, much like the one you're at, just beyond the park. You can look down on the park and see the network of paths, all intricately wound together to access the different parts of the park.

The people and the bushes now look small and blurry, unimportant in the overall spectacle before you. Up, up you go, you become aware that there is another city, it doesn't look terribly far away from here, you can see it on the horizon. Between the two cities is an extensive railroad and highway system, crossing a wide river on magnificent bridges, none of which you could see before.

Up and up you go, you can see the curvature of the earth. Miles and miles in every direction, you become aware of mountains and lakes that you didn't know were there previously. You reach the top floor and step out onto the roof of the building. All the while, reveling in all that you are now aware of and all of which was always there, beyond your perception at ground level, all the intricate connections and vastness of the world in which we live. Just then, a plane sounds overhead. As you look up, far above, you can just make out a face in the window, looking down upon you, as the plane climbs above the clouds.

I hope now you can see why awareness is important with regard to expanding our minds, being open to new ideas, people, places, and things. Our brains actually filter out much of what is going on around us, if you can believe that.

Think about this, what if, each moment of everyday, you were aware of every sight, sound, color, smell, or sensation. You would probably lose your mind from the overload of information to the brain. To combat this, the brain has a small pencil-sized network of nerve pathways known as the reticular formation.

This network of nerve pathways connecting the spinal cord, cerebrum and cerebellum together are called the Reticular Activating System (RAS). The reticular activating system acts as a gatekeeper of information between our sensory systems and the conscious mind. It filters out unnecessary information so that the important stuff gets through. The RAS also seeks information that validates our beliefs.

Consider this, if you were aware of everything in your surroundings, all the time, you would have a brain melt down. It is just too many bits of information. The RAS filters this out so your brain only pays attention to what you deem to be important, everything else melts into the background or just seems like it's not there.

A classic example of this is you go to a car dealership in search of a new car. You don't have anything in particular in mind, but as you are perusing the aisles, a red honda civic pops out and catches your attention. Now you may not have noticed this car before, but you are open minded as you are in need of a new car. You think to yourself, wow, what a great looking car, haven't seen one of those before? In talking with the salesman he informs you they are a very popular model, one of his biggest sellers.

Strange, you think to yourself, thought I would have seen more around if they are that popular. You purchase the car and drive home. After a few days, you start seeing a car just like yours here and there, your neighbor down the street has one and a guy from work, two cubicles down, also owns one. All of a sudden, you realize that there are red Honda Civics everywhere.

Now, All of these cars did not just show up, you must be pretty ego centered to think that everyone ran out and bought a car just like you did. These cars were there all along, you were just filtering them out because they weren't important to you, you had no need to acknowledge them, but now that's your car, and we need to be able to find it in the parking lot at the mall. Now, we look at it and look for it every day, it is very important to us, this is how the Reticular Activating System works.

Similarly, that is how the RAS seeks information to validate our beliefs. By filtering out what is unimportant to us and only allowing information we deem important, our beliefs and biases are often supported. If you hold the belief that old people are mean, for instance, the RAS will filter out 10 older ladies smiling and being cordial but you will certainly notice the man with the cane being short and gruff with the cashier then next line over at the grocery store.

That may be a bit of a simplistic example on both accounts of how the RAS works. I think it is sufficient to say that when you bring into your awareness that this is occurring, through self awareness, what your inner emotions and beliefs are, you will see how different ideas, thoughts and opportunities will begin to show up that previously had been filtered out.

Awareness is key to growth. It can be very refreshing, eye opening, and inspiring when we gain awareness in any of our three areas, environmental, self, and spiritual. So much so that typically, once someone has begun to raise their self and spiritual awareness, they feel compelled to share it with others. They want to help them become more aware and to explore that which was previously unknown, beyond reach or sight. I know this to be true, as that is one of the many reasons why I feel so compelled to share what I am aware of with you.

LESSON #7

Gratitude is Essential

∽

*"Gratitude is the healthiest of all human emotions.
The more you express gratitude for what you have,
the more likely you will have even more to express gratitude for."*
—Zig Zigler

Gratitude is hands down the most important practice that one can adopt in their lives. If the only thing that you implement from this book is an understanding and daily practice of gratitude, you will see astounding changes in your mental attitude, your interactions with others, and the amount of 'Good Stuff' that will enter your life.

Gratitude is quite simply the quality of being thankful, the readiness to show appreciation, and to return kindness. 'Derived' from the latin word, gratus, which embodied the concept of pleasing/thankful. Gratitude is a feeling of appreciation. Practicing gratitude has many benefits.

Those who make gratitude a daily practice by taking time to notice and reflect upon the things they are thankful for, experience more positive emotions. They also feel more alive, more compassionate, and even experience strengthened immune systems.

Gratitude is the most basic foundation for personal and spiritual growth. To be thankful for what we have on a regular basis is the fastest, most complete way to view the people and circumstances in your life differently.

When we complain to others about people, possessions, circumstances in our lives or the lack thereof, this is the opposite of gratitude. The opposite of gratitude can be characterized by dissatisfaction or unappreciation. The more we complain about the people and things in our lives that we don't like, the more of these things we attract to us. Additionally, we present ourselves to those around us as helpless, frustrated victims of circumstances beyond our control. Not a very powerful way to represent yourself to the world around you.

Along with that, comes the prevalence for heart and digestive issues, among a host of other health issues. As we find ourselves in a continuous state of anxiety over the very things we wish would change, we try to feel some relief from the stress of our family, our job, our financial status, the bills, our health issues, and so on.

The truth is, no amount of wishing, complaining or blaming will help any of these matters. Often we have become addicted to these low energy vibration thoughts and behaviors, making matters even worse. We cannot even imagine that there is anything different for ourselves.

I know this, because I too, found myself experiencing those very things years ago. The worst was during the time of my divorce, it was an especially low period in my life. It was so easy to get into a 'Woe as me' frame of mind and without awareness of what I was projecting, I received more of the same. In that state, you can see that other people have it differently, more money, more love, better relationships, a better outlook on life, more luck in business. To view life through the lens of dissatisfaction can indeed make things seem hopeless.

This is where gratitude comes in as the number one game changer. Though it may be a challenge at first, especially if you find yourself dwelling in the depths described above. Fear not, as help is on the way. The physical act of being grateful for what is in your life is what turns the tides and begins your mental, emotional, and vibrational ascension.

For starters, it is impossible to hold anxious thoughts in your mind when you are focused on that which you are grateful for. So, if you feel an anxious thought entering: "I am not sure I can pay my phone bill, it's due next week." Head it off with a thought of gratitude: "I am so grateful for my phone, life would be less enjoyable without this miraculous device, I am lucky to live in a time of such incredible technology that helps me stay connected so easily." After all, so much of that is true and we tend to find money to afford the things that are really important to us.

You can see the difference in these two lines of thinking. One is based on fear of the future, inadequacy, and views the phone bill as a burden that must be shouldered, even at the cost of personal wellbeing. The second, free of fear. An expression of the awe and appreciation that you truly have, day to day for this amazing tool in your life. Surely the money agreed upon to possess and operate this indispensable personal device is a pittance compared to the value you get from it.

This is the essence of gratitude, when practiced, it is a simple, beautiful way to rewire your brain. A powerful tool to quiet and head off those habitual, anxious thoughts that plague so many of us and rob us of our joy and freedom.

One can find an almost endless amount of memes, quotes and information on the power and practice of gratitude online. As with many of our other lessons, its simplicity allows a great deal of customization and whatever practice you adopt, it should feel real and authentic to you, not just a written routine where you are going through the motions. You've got to feel it!

The first opportunity each day to express gratitude is right when you wake up in the morning. We are just coming out of the theta brain wave state, the dreamlike state when we are most susceptible we talked about in lesson five. This is the best time of the day to begin that rewiring process.

Simply, have gratitude for being alive to experience a new day, roughly 150,000 people won't get that opportunity worldwide, each day. So be thankful. "Thank you for this day, it is going to be amazing" or "Thank you for this new day and all the good things coming to me."

Again, you must figure out what is right for you, these are just suggestions to get you started. As with any practice or learning process, this may feel silly or strange at the beginning. That's okay, just stick with it and keep trying. The second best time for gratitude and you will see this recurring theme due to the entrance and exit of Theta state, is to give thanks right before you fall asleep at night. To lay there in your bed, comfortable and relaxed, think about all the things you are thankful for.

Keep it simple, don't feel pressure to make it extravagant. "I am so grateful for my warm bed, my house, my spouse, my children, my dog" and so on. Lay there, feeling the feeling of gratitude for those things in your life that are important. This will be something you will look forward to each day.

Verbalizing your gratitude to yourself and others is a great way to stay elevated and keep a positive mindset throughout the day. You may even surprise yourself after a while, telling family and co-workers just how thankful you are that they are in your life.

As easy and helpful verbal gratitude is in getting the positive mindset-ball rolling. I must stress the importance of the following exercise. I have seen it done many different ways, again different strokes for different folks. I am going to illustrate what works for me and why.

My daily practice of gratitude was adopted from the PGI coaching program with Bob Proctor and Sandy Gallagher. It is a simple exercise to perform, but they stressed to me— and I will stress to you—the importance of precision in your phrasing.

The exercise is simply to write out ten things that you are thankful for each day. Sounds easy enough, right? It is important to write this out in a gratitude journal, just as taking notes in class is important for imprinting information on the brain, so is writing in the gratitude journal. This can be a simple notebook, what is important is each line of gratitude must be written in the present tense. This is because the subconscious mind cannot differentiate between what is real and what is not.

The subconscious mind always says, "Yes." It cannot tell whether you are actually running a race or watching one on TV. Give it things to say yes to, that you want.

Always write gratitude and affirmations in the present tense, as if you already possess it. In Addition, you must make an "I am" statement. "I am" statements are powerful, definitive statements. A clear command to yourself and the universe. Not I want, not I think, not I guess, I AM!

Here are some examples that I use for writing gratitude. First I use what I refer to as a gratitude anchor as my first line or two. For me, I am very thankful for my fiance, Joni, she is always very supportive of me and someone I am unquestioningly grateful for in my life. This is the feeling you should use as a gratitude anchor, no matter what it is, for you.

"I am so Happy and Grateful now that Joni is in my life and our love grows each day."

Now, this is a statement that I easily and readily feel is true for me, hence the reason it is an anchor, to get a hold of the feeling of gratitude. The elements that are important in this statement are the "I am" and the "Now that" placing it in the present tense. It is imperative to include these two elements in the gratitude writing.

Using this technique you can also be grateful for things that have not yet shown up, because it is written in present tense, your subconscious mind thinks that it is here already and makes it easier for you to believe as well, which is an important part of 'being ready to receive.'

Statements can be as general or specific as you choose. You should write down what feels right. It is not necessary to write out the same things each day, but you can keep some the same for a while. Here is a fairly generic one I use often: "I am so happy and grateful now that money comes to me easily and frequently." It's simple, open-ended, everyone wants it.

If I can, at that time, open my wallet and look at some money, touch it, acknowledge its truth or think about a check coming to me in the mail, then that all the more solidifies that feeling of thankfulness.

As you begin to look for and acknowledge those things in your life that you already have and are thankful for, something else amazing happens. Remember the Reticular Activating System from the last chapter? It starts identifying and paying attention to that which you deem important. Red Honda Civics, yes, but it is also seeking information to validate your beliefs. If you believe on a fundamental level that you have many things to be grateful for, it will seek out more things for which you can be grateful.

Pretty cool, huh? Practice gratitude daily, follow the instructions carefully and I guarantee you will be absolutely amazed with the growth in your own life, and in turn those around you. After all, gratitude is very contagious, so spread that good stuff around, and more is sure to follow. I, for one, am so happy and grateful now that you are manifesting the life of your dreams.

LESSON #8

Forgiveness is Freedom

∽

*"Forgiveness is the fragrance that
the violet sheds on the heel that has crushed it."*
—Mark Twain

What exactly is forgiveness and why is it important?

Forgiveness is a conscious, deliberate decision to release feelings of resentment or vengeance toward a person or a group who has harmed you, regardless of whether they actually deserve your forgiveness. Forgiveness does not mean forgetting, nor does it mean condoning or excusing offenses.

For me, forgiveness was always something a bit misunderstood, I have found out that I was not alone in this. As a child, I was always told to "forgive your sister" for some wrongdoing or that someone would forgive me for a mistake I made, usually all this took was a simple: "I'm sorry." Boom, done.

As I got older I started to pick up on different information about forgiveness and what it really means. I think that my understanding of forgiveness over the years was basically that you forgave someone so that they could stop feeling bad about wronging you. If someone showed remorse about some wrongdoing, of which you were the recipient. They would repent and say. "I'm sorry, please forgive me," then you would grant them forgiveness.

This seems to be the model most portrayed by the catholic church, while I am not Catholic, I always seemed to have a firm grasp of 'confession,' perhaps due to TV and movies, where the priest in the confession box asks you to admit and repent your sins. Once you have done that, he gives you however many 'Hail Mary's' he thinks you deserve, then he grants forgiveness and the repentant no longer has to feel guilty about their sins. Right?

Come to find out, forgiveness is far more complex and powerful. It is the healing agent for the mind, body and emotional self.

First of all, it can be difficult to properly forgive or to forgive at all. Many of us carry long standing grudges, some we may not even be aware of, that over time, we find harder and harder to let go. I personally fell into this category, so I can attest to the frustration and deep seated anger that harboring feelings like this towards another person or situation in your life can be. It is literally like dragging a boat anchor around, it is exhausting.

The next section here is from *Psycho Cybernetics* by Maxwell Maltz. An amazing book, a must read for anyone interested in personal development. Maxwell Maltz was a psychiatrist and a plastic surgeon, this provided for an interesting perspective in his studies of the human condition and some of the driving forces behind our behaviors. His observations and conclusions are truly thought provoking and educational.

A primary lesson taken from Mr. Maltz is that we find it hard to forgive because we like a sense of condemnation, we enjoy nursing our wounds to keep them open, like picking a scab so the wound won't heal. It makes us feel superior to those that hurt us.

This was a real eye opener for me. I had never heard a concept like this before. Was it true?

As I examined my thoughts and behaviors, to my suprise, I found that there was an element of superiority present. I found that there was a nursing of those old wounds that would get brought up each time the occasion offered. This was surely an insight worth exploring. If you find that this is true for you as well, you are not alone, trust me, it will feel great to let go.

Foregiveness's function is not for us to feel good at any given moment, it's supposed to allow us to be happy. Forgiveness does not make us superior, nor is it supposed to be revenge. Forgiveness is supposed to be like spiritual surgery, to give up grudges like one would give up a gangrenous arm. You would certainly not hang on to a gangrenous arm, a diseased, dangerous appendage, no longer functioning properly and sure to spread to the rest of the body with fatal results.

Holding a grudge is much the same, it does not benefit you nor hurt the person it is held against, we have all heard the saying, "Resentment is like drinking poison and waiting for the other person to die." I hope you can agree that none of us want to be so foolish in our personal development to fall into that category. So how do we avoid that trap and make a better choice?

In raising our conscious awareness, the logical next step is to look at the positive aspects of forgiveness and the most effective way to forgive ourselves and others in our lives. Forgiveness is like a cancelled bank note, never to be brought up again. Partial forgiveness will not help, your forgiveness itself, must be forgotten, as well as the wrong which needed forgiveness. Do not forgive for prideful or vengeful reasons, they miss the mark. In therapeutic forgiveness, we forgive because we have come to recognize that the debt itself is not valid.

Oftentimes, the person with which we withhold our forgiveness, has no knowledge of their crime against you, and if they do, they are unable to undo or fix that wrong doing anyway, as that time has passed and can never be revisited. True forgiveness comes only when we are able to see and emotionally accept that there is and was nothing for us to forgive. We should not have condemned or hated the person in the first place, as we do not have the power nor the right to condemn another.

Now we have an idea about the importance of forgiving others and why it is important. As mentioned above there is another matter to attend to, that can be more challenging, it is forgiveness of yourself. That's right, you must forgive yourself for any past transgressions. Did you even realize that you were holding a grudge against yourself?

Simply put, we need to acknowledge and recognize our own errors and mistakes. The purpose of us all, in this life is to explore, experience, learn and grow. You would not hold a grudge against a child for spilling the milk, how long will you hold a grudge against yourself for a mistake?

Emotions are used correctly and appropriately when they help us to respond to some reality in the present environment. Since we cannot live in the past, we cannot appropriately respond to past events emotionally. We do not need to take an emotional position, one way or the other, regarding detours that might have taken us off course in the past. We beat ourselves over the head with condemnation, remorse and regret. We beat ourselves down with self doubt, cut ourselves to the bone with guilt, I have been there myself. It does not serve us. Remorse and regret are attempts to emotionally live in the past, excessive guilt is to make right something in the past we did or thought was wrong, neither will help or serve us.

It is futile and fatal to hate or condemn ourselves for our past mistakes, we need to be our own biggest supporter, kind and understanding. The sooner we are able to begin forgiving ourselves and feeling that weight lift off our shoulders, from no longer carrying that burden of guilt, that chip the size of an elephant.

The sooner and more easily we can begin to cut away that gangrenous arm of resentment towards others as well. As we speak to ourselves, so shall we speak to others. I would personally like to thank Mr. Maltz for that powerful lesson, it has made a huge transformation in my life and I have little doubt it will for you as well. I would like to leave you with the timeless wisdom so eloquently portrayed here is this Buddhist prayer of forgiveness, may it serve you well in the future.

> If I have harmed anyone in anyway,
>
> either knowingly or unknowingly,
>
> through my own confusion,
>
> I ask their forgiveness,
>
> if anyone has harmed me in anyway,
>
> either knowingly or unknowingly,
>
> through their own confusions,
>
> I forgive them,
>
> and if there is a situation,
>
> I am not ready to forgive,
>
> I forgive myself for that,
>
> for all the ways that I harm myself,
>
> negate, doubt, belittle myself,
>
> judge or be unkind to myself,
>
> through my confusions,
>
> I forgive myself.

LESSON #9

Attitude is Everything

⌒∞⌒

What a great saying. I am sure we have all heard it before. It was actually the slogan at my high school in 1995, but what does it really mean? I can be sure that not many of us knew back in '95.

First let's start by defining 'attitude' so we can all be on the same page conceptually. Attitude is defined as a settled way of thinking or feeling about someone or something, typically one that is reflected in a person's behavior.

So, to be more clear, an attitude is thoughts or feelings that reflect themselves in a person's behavior. OK. Why is this important? Why could our thoughts and feelings reflected in our behavior be everything?

One reason this is important is because your attitude is how you engage the world around you. It not only affects you but the people around you. Have you ever encountered a person you perceived to have a great or winning attitude? How did it make you feel to be around that person?

Now, Have you ever been around someone that had a poor attitude or was self defeating? How did it make you feel to be around a person like that? We have all been there and I have little doubt that we have stood in the shoes of both these examples at one time or another.

We are all capable of having both a positive and negative attitude, either outwardly or inwardly. Why would we choose a negative attitude?

Our Thoughts and feelings, especially about ourselves, are a culmination of our experience and our perceptions of those experiences. We are a reflection of our parents, our families, our communities. We are literally programmed by these things in the first seven years of life according to Dr. Bruce Lipton, he goes on to state that after the age of 7, 95% of the results in your life come from the programming of the subconscious mind. If we are unaware of how this program is affecting us, many of us are totally unaware that we even HAVE a negative, self defeating attitude. I was one of these people. Since I talked like and thought like the people around me, in general the people surrounding me agreed or had similar thoughts and feelings, then I did not question whether I had a negative attitude or not.

The real kicker is that when you have a self-defeating attitude, you tend to attract others with the same attitude. It is said that you are the culmination of the five people that you spend the most time with. Wrap your head around that for a while.

If you are surrounded by like-minded people, displaying a negative attitude and you come across a person with a positive attitude, in general you will not want to be around that person or hear what they have to say. One may even criticize that person in an attempt to bring them into more familiar territory.

Now, I tell you this, not as a judgement. I believe that we are all doing the best we are able at the time with the circumstances and information we have available to us, regardless of how we come off to others.

My point is that awareness is necessary to first see the flaws in our attitude, mind you this is something that generally does not change overnight but gradually or in small leaps and bounds as it is practiced, as is the case with most types of growth.

Once a person becomes aware that they are reflecting a negative attitude, they have a choice. They can either continue saying, "Well, that's just the way I am, people can't change" or they can decide to adopt a new attitude which involves changing the thoughts and feelings that are reflected in the person's actions and behaviors.

There are so many great teachers about this subject, but I would like to highlight one of my favorites here, Dr. Wayne Dyer.

Dr. Dyer, who is no longer with us, was a spiritual master and teacher that lived on the island of Maui, Hawaii and has over 30 published works to his name, each of them truly a piece of inspiration. A man so humble and human despite his great knowledge and achievements, even this great spiritual teacher would give himself daily reminders about his choice of attitude each day when he left his house. An affirmation that hung on his door said, "Attitude is everything, so pick a good one."

This is a reminder that attitude is not something we choose once but that it is a choice we make each day, all throughout our day, because not everything is going to go according to your plans or be just the way you thought it would be, or shall stay the way our 'Ego-selves' want it to be.

Our 'Ego-selves,' the part of us that is in control when we are on autopilot, not living in the present moment with conscious awareness, wants to feel like it is in control, and when it is not, that can disrupt us and cause us to react. This is a sure fire way to reflect a bad attitude.

A better way is to RESPOND with kindness in all situations, at first this is easier said than done, and let's remember that true nobility, as Dr. Dyer reminds us, is not being better than anyone else, but to be better than we were yesterday.

To be a better version of ourselves each day and therefore choose a progressively better attitude for ourselves, what can we do?

In order to change our thoughts and feelings to reflect a better attitude, we can first and foremost choose kindness in all situations, towards ourselves and others. Yes, you read that right. Most important is kindness to yourself, when you practice kindness towards yourself it will automatically translate into kindness to others.

To facilitate kindness to yourself, it helps to begin with an attitude of gratitude, to give thanks for all that is in your experience, without judgement, can be a powerful tool to perceiving and interacting with the world differently.

Remind yourself, each day, that you are a piece of God, a piece of the creator, a receiver of infinite intelligence. Remember to live 'in Spirit,' as you are an infinite spiritual being living a temporary human experience. A ghost in the machine, let that infinite intelligence, that spirit be the driving force of your machine, not the autopilot that was programmed in the first seven years. That may have served you in the morning of your life but now is a time to allow. To allow that spiritual being to flow and flourish.

The Ego wants to own and control, to blame and to hate, to be seperate from. These are the precursors to a 'bad' attitude.

Spirit, God, Source, wants to love, to create, to give without judgement, without need for repayment.

Dr. Dyer quotes the Persion poet, Hafez, in his 2009 Movie: 'The Shift' on the spiritual meaning of Love. "Even after all this time, the Sun never says to the Earth, you owe me. Look at what happens with a love like that, it lights the whole sky."

What a beautiful metaphor for the love we are all capable of, and how that kind of attitude can light up the world around us.

To help us reach a level such as Hafez foresaw we may also turn to another great teacher, also a favorite of Dr. Dyer, his name is Lao Tzu. He was a chinese spiritual master that lived in the 4th century BC. Though he lived many centuries ago, his lessons still ring true today. The lessons are called the Four Cardinal Virtues or rules for living.

The first of these Cardinal Virtues was Reverence for all life, we should respect all forms of creation and not seek to dominate or control them, but first we must honor and love ourselves. Then this love will flow outwardly toward all beings. In this world, we must depend on other life forms for our sheer survival. This means that we must treat them with respect, kindness and gratitude.

Next, is natural Sincerity. This virtue manifests itself as honesty, simplicity and authenticity. It basically states to stay true to who you really are and not allow outside influences to sway you. Own your true nature and don't let others tell you who to be.

Once we can come from a place of realness and sincerity, we can begin to understand what we need to remain happy and peaceful and we can extend this to include others who might struggle along their path as well. Live your truth and everything else will fall into place. Doing so will inspire others along the way to also show their true selves and live authentically. Allow your thoughts and your actions to align and you'll come to know the meaning of sincerity.

The third virtue is gentleness, for in the world we live today, we really need this virtue to be practiced more often. Gentleness means simply being kind to all life and not coming from a place of Egoistic desires. When we practice gentleness, we give up the need to be right, because being kind is more important than being correct.

When we're sensitive to other people's needs and throw away the desire to control or dominate them, we can live in harmony with one another. Many people mistake being gentle and kind as being weak, but this is only because we live in a world of inflated Egos. Practice gentleness and you'll awaken yourself in the world to what truly matters.

The last virtue is supportiveness, this one implies that we must support all life forms, including ourselves. When we first attend to supporting ourselves, we can more easily help others we encounter along our life's journey. This final Cardinal Virtue states to love and serve all, regardless of what we can get from it. We can shift from a place of wanting to receive into a place of giving without wondering what we will get in return. This virtue comes natural to us as children but this world we've been born into tells us to focus on ourselves to become happier. In reality, many people do not feel fulfilled following this path. So, by putting ourselves aside and living to serve others, we may find a life of true purpose and joy by striving to make other peoples lives a little easier.

So, begin practicing these four virtues today, notice how much more graceful and easy you can move through your day. Bringing to you those things that you give away in ever greater abundance. Daily practice of these virtues and the lessons they hold can help you to shed destructive, self-defeating patterns that sabotage your inner sense of happiness and peace.

Surely once practices such as these are implemented, a shift in attitude is the only possibility, and by doing so, you will affect both the people and the world around you. More and more you will feel inspired to share what you know with others, you will attract the good that you give without thought of reciprocation or reward and just being in the presence of others will raise their awareness of what is possible within themselves. Truly, you will be a better version of yourself today than you were yesterday and remember, that is the true definition of nobility.

Indeed, attitude is everything, be sure and pick a good one. Thank you, Dr. Dyer, may your wise words echo into eternity!

LESSON #10

Follow Your Intuition

(THAT GUIDING VOICE FROM WITHIN)

A hunch, premonition, second sight, clairvoyance, sixth sense, mothers intuition. Do these sound familiar? We have all heard these labels before, and may even have some idea of what they are. It's not just others that possess intuition, we all possess intuition, but what is it?

Intuition is the ability to acquire knowledge without recourse to conscious reasoning. The word 'Intuition' has a great variety of meanings, ranging from direct access to unconscious knowledge, unconscious cognition, inner sensing, inner insight to unconscious pattern recognition. Along with the ability to understand something instinctively, without the need for conscious reasoning.

To call it instinct may be a little simplistic as we humans are capable of so much more than our animal friends, but I have little doubt that they are similar. Intuition is an inner knowing, you may not even be sure how you know, but you know.

Instinct leads birds to migrate, tells them when to leave and when to return, for many birds, they return to the very spot where they themselves hatched from the egg, to lay their own. Is that memory or instinct, are they related?

Intuition does come from the primitive brain, it is an artifact of the early days of man, when the brain's ability to detect hidden dangers ensured our survival. These days, so seldom do we use this capability, we have not learned to use it properly. We are taught to listen to reason, listen to authority and not necessarily to that small voice from within.

Though I found many different descriptions of intuition and categories, to keep it simple, to gain understanding, I want to share the four types presented by author Michelle Depres in her book: *"Intuitively You, Evolve Your Life and Mend The World."*

Depres tells us that intuition is a way to use our core instincts to find better solutions to life's issues. She breaks intuition down into four categories as follows:

1. **Clairvoyance**: The intuitive act of clear seeing. This is 'The flash in the mind's eye' when you have a vision of a future event that happens later. It may be an image or scene that suddenly appears in your mind, sometimes in the form of a day dream. This intuitive prompting can sometimes act as a warning device, foretelling events like auto accidents or cause you to think of an old friend who then suddenly calls you out of the blue.

2. **Clairaudience**: The intuitive act of clear hearing. This is the ability to sense 'frequency' resonance and vibrations 'within' you. This most commonly appears as a voice you hear that's not coming from someone that is physically present. You may hear a warning or receive guidance from a parent, living or deceased, as well as other authority figures, including spirit guides.

3. **Clairsentience**: The intuitive act of clear sensing. This is feeling emotions or sensations, that includes the energy of those around you. You might suddenly feel sad, because you are standing next to someone who is depressed. This can be positive or negative depending on your point of view, because it gives you the ability to sense and help others in need.

4. **Claircognizance**: The intuitive act of clear knowing. This is an instantaneous knowledge that can appear as instinct. It is said to be the equivalent of a light turning on. You come across a problem and immediately know the solution, even though you've given it no real thought. Another example is you know immediately if a person you just met is either genuine or dishonest.

I found these four basic categories to be imperative and relevant. I know that when I looked through the definitions, I had a feeling of which ones described my experiences of intuition, as I have come to know it, as I am sure certain ones resonated more with you than others. We must remember that all people are different when it comes to the levels of consciousness and awareness in which we are functioning.

I can tell you from personal experience that I was taught to listen to what I was told, no one ever instructed me to listen to my gut. For many years I resisted what my inner knowing was telling me to be true, that way lies madness. Just like a limb that has been put in a cast or a sling, so is your intuition, it is like a muscle. When used regularly, focused upon, can be exercised and tuned so that we have great strength and control.

But when left idle, like an arm in a sling, it becomes atrophied, weak and lethargic. The more you allow that inner voice to guide you, the more you can trust that inner knowing, the better it can serve you and in turn make you more effective in your own life.

Now, let's take a moment and clarify between your inner intuitive knowing and the cautious voice of fear. That cautious voice of fear which presents itself so loudly is not your intuition. That is likely a paradigm or a terror barrier developed over time, that is your reasoning brain, we will discuss that more in depth, further down the line.

For now, remember this. Fear will turn you away from your innermost desires, while your intuition is guiding you towards the life of your dreams. Manage your fear with reason, if you can see a rational, real, clear situation to be cautious, respect it and make sound choices. If there is no clear, tangible reason for fear to be present and your inner voice is calling to you to do something, even if it doesn't make sense, go for it. Infinite intelligence knows your path better than you do.

In my research to learn more about intuition and what it really is, I found something truly amazing. Something that is both ancient and at the leading edge of spirituality that is backed by science.

The first comes from the Heart Math institute and Gregg Braden. In 1991, scientists discovered 40,000 brain-like cells in the heart, dubbed 'The little brain in the heart.' These 40,000 cells called 'sensory neurons' think independently from the brain but are also neurologically connected to the cerebral brain. Each experience we have is registered in both the heart and the brain. Traumas especially can lodge in the brain and the heart. Whereas, the brain can be healed through counseling and logical choice, the trauma may still be 'lodged' in the 'heart-brain,' hence the term "mending a broken heart."

Every culture on the planet traditionally understands the role the heart plays in the human condition. When we point to ourselves, we point to our heart, nowhere else. This is the seat of our soul, the core of our existence. After all, our first organ to develop as an embryo is the heart, its appearance is the seed of life and the final beat of that heart is the signal of transition for the body that the spirit is moving on.

Heart intelligence points to our sensory neurons that are linked to an intelligence that is right for you. Your own personal guidance system, built literally into the heart of your being. According to Gregg Braden, you can access this knowledge by taking a quiet moment, slowing down your breathing, this tells your brain and body that you are safe and open to guidance. Touching your fingertips to your heart, ask a single clear question. The heart will instantly know the answer that is right for you. Trust your heart, trust your intuition.

The heart differs from the brain when asked for information. The brain is a polarity organ, it has a right side and a left side, each with its own function and point of view. These opposing sides of the organ can cause confusion as each side jockeys for domination. We have all experienced this tennis match of indecision. The heart however is a 'whole' organ that is 'of one mind.' Literally this 'little brain in the heart' has been with us since day one, it was instrumental in the development of your being, which should speak volumes about its ability to guide you on tough decisions where no one path appears more beneficial than the other.

As fascinating as it is to learn about 'the little brain in the heart,' which there is a great deal of information and scientific study to explore on the subject, there is something else worth mentioning.

Ever experience butterflies in your stomach when you were nervous or a stomach ache when you felt anxious? Turns out that there are also brain cells all the way down in your digestive tract, though it sounds incredible, it kinda makes sense. Haven't you ever heard of listening to your gut? This is called the Enteric nervous system, which mirrors the central nervous system. These two brains are interconnected, so when one gets upset, the other does too.

The Enteric nervous system is located in the sheaths of the tissue lining the esophagus, stomach, small intestine and colon. Considered a single entity, it is a network of neurons, neurotransmitters and proteins that zap messages between neurons, support cells like that found in the brain proper and a complex circuitry that enables it to act independently, learn, remember and as the saying goes, produce gut feelings. Our bodies are certainly incredible indeed.

Additionally, according to Dr. Gershon, who is considered one of the founders of a new field of medicine called Neurogastroenterology, nearly every substance that helps run and control the brain has turned up in the gut. Major neurotransmitters like Serotonin, Dopamine, Glutamate, Norepinephrine, and Nitric Oxide are there as well. Two dozen small brain proteins, called neuropeptides are in the gut as are major cells of the immune system.

While this is all amazing information, it is not all that surprising when you think about the human body as an energetic system, interconnected and dependent on each major system to act both independently and as a whole.

Eastern philosophy has known this for millenia, the chakra system, the independent sources of energy or chi in the body. The chakras are thought to vitalize the body and to be associated with interactions of our physical, mental and emotional nature. The function of the chakras is to spin and draw in the energies of the body and keep the spiritual, mental, physical and emotional health of the body in balance.

So, we can see that there is both new scientific evidence and ancient spiritual knowledge of thought systems and centers in the body, where thought activity, independent from the reasoning mind of the cerebral brain occurs. Our intuition, that guiding voice from within stems from these additional thought centers, not just figments of our imagination but real, tangible, scientific reality.

Now that we are armed with some new information about our intuition, the different categories of its use and the source of these thoughts and feelings, let's look at some practical ways to access this guiding voice from within.

Here are three practical exercises to help aid in creating a deeper relationship with your inner self, clarifying that inner voice and allow you to bring back your instinctual awareness that may have been lying dormant.

1. You can keep a journal, writing your thoughts down, even if they are small quiet thoughts. Writing can help your subconscious mind flow

2. Turn off that inner critic, this is something that can quiet that intuitive inner voice that seeks to guide you. That inner critic which speaks so loudly. Politely set that critic aside, within yourself and let the wisdom of your gut instinct take center stage.

3. As you are developing the awareness and trust in your inner guidance system, be sure and find a quiet, private, safe place where you can allow your thoughts and emotions to flow freely without judgement by others.

These small steps, though they may not seem like much, can make a huge impact not only with regard to your own inner knowing, but in the trust and confidence that it can build up within you. After all, confidence is belief in yourself, the ability to trust your own instincts and intuition in any situation despite a lack of rational thought or lack of information, requires you to act. This is where the superstars among us get that edge. Businessmen, star athletes, first responders, anyone that must act in the moment and trust wholly in their decisions is connected to these places inside. Connected to the heart, to the gut, to that intuitive knowing within that never steers you wrong. That 'Little brain in the heart' that is forever unwavering, guiding you down the path that leads to the life of your dreams, follow it, trust it. We are all so blessed to possess such amazing guidance systems in this crazy world, use them well.

LESSON #11

Visualization:

It's Not Just Daydreaming Anymore!

∽

Do you remember daydreaming as a kid, sitting in class or at home with your homework in front of you, staring off into space? In your mind you were somewhere else, off on an adventure or playing outside on the swings in your mind because it was a beautiful day. I am reminded of the comic strip: *Calvin and Hobbes* by Bill Watterson. In the strip, which ran for well over a decade starting in the mid-1980's, Calvin is depicted as a perpetual six-year-old boy and his stuffed tiger.

In Calvin's mind, the tiger was real and they would always have amazing adventures, without ever really leaving their mundane, suburban cul de sac lives. In Calvin's imagination he could turn an ordinary box into a time machine to take himself and Hobbes back to the Jurassic or flip the box around and have it then be a transmogrifier to turn himself into a tiger.

Calvin could visualize himself sitting at his desk in school and all of a sudden, growing bigger and bigger until he had outgrown the school, outgrew his town, outgrew his country and eventually until he was so large that he fell off the earth it was so small and he was floating in the milky way galaxy.

Like Calvin, we all spent the first years of our lives in a dreamlike state, the Theta state is the primary state of brain wave activity in our lives until the age of seven, it is a precious and magical time. The seamless transition between the world right in front of them and the 'reality' they see in their minds. In the child's mind a broom handle becomes a horse in the fantasy they are playing out, to the point where they will argue adamantly with whomever doesn't see it the way that they do.

Simply an amazing and powerful tool, the imagination. It has been found that adolescent chimpanzees, not quite ready to mate, will break away from the mother to carry a special stick or a rock on their backs, rocking, cradling and nurturing it as if it is their baby. This points to the ability of the chimps to 'imagine' that this object is its baby. This ability to imagine is clearly something innate to our deep ancestral roots.

As magical and useful as these creative powers of visualization are, unfortunately at some point, we were taught to snap out of it. Stop daydreaming and come back to reality to 'get real.' For many of us we lost those abilities to visualize, to imagine things that weren't there, the ability to create anything we chose in our minds. It was deemed unimportant and discouraged, like any skill or muscle, when unused, they fade away. Truly sad.

Luckily, not all of us were good listeners, there have always been the stubborn few, on the fringe, steadfastly clinging to their visions. Once just ordinary people like you and me, they are now known to history as our visionaries. Nikola Tesla, Thomas Edison, Henry Ford, Rosa Parks, Martin Luther King, Steve Jobs, Amelia Airhart, Elon Musk, the list goes on and on. These are the people of vision. They could see the world not just as it is but as they wanted it to be, and were willing to hold their vision with conviction until the two worlds became one. Oftentimes, this vision was so powerful that they were able to get others to see their crazy daydreams and help bring them to fruition.

The truth is that without our powers of visualization, there would be none of the things in our world that we are familiar with today, we would still be living in the trees, if that is really where we came from in the first place. Every human invention, past, present and future originated in the imagination. Likewise all of our most egregious atrocities began as an idea, an image in the mind. So this power is not to be regarded or used lightly.

> *"Whatever the mind of man can conceive and believe,*
> *it can achieve."*
> —Napoleon Hill

What I have found is that some people struggle to visualize. Typically, it is because they just haven't done it for so long, it feels foreign, strange or silly. For others it feels like the most natural thing to do, often these are our artists and inventors, designers, architects and photographers. They see it first in their mind, then they set forth into action to create it and bring it into our world.

Please remember that we all have the ability to visualize. For those that do struggle with it, I would like to bring to your attention a book Co-Authored by a friend of mine, Lloyd Chambers. Lloyd and his co-author, Jackie Carrol in their recently published book: *Visualisation to Realisation*, chronicles their individual and collective journeys to building the life of their dreams using the power of visualization along with other useful creative faculties. This can be helpful for those that want to learn more about developing these skills.

It also reveals Jackie Carrol as a pioneer and champion for those struggling to visualize as she has set out to develop a virtual reality simulation system, so that anyone can readily visualize the life of their dreams. The technology is right around the corner and Jackie's imagination and visualization is being put to work to help bring it into reality, in turn, yours will be as well. Fantastic stuff.

Another great teacher that has had loads of success using visualization, among many others, is Jack Canfield, best known as one of the creators of the *Chicken Soup for The Soul* series of books. Featured in the film, 'The Secret,' he discusses how he used his powers of visualization to jumpstart his career. In the film he told a story of how he used a $100,000 bill that he made himself to be a reminder to visualize a new life that previously seemed beyond his reach.

Jim Carey used a similar technique with a check that he wrote to himself for ten million dollars and even dated it, carrying it with him for years so that he saw it every time he opened his wallet. At the time he was just an aspiring actor and comedian without any real prospects trying to find his place in Hollywood. He would even go so far as to drive up into the Hollywood Hills as if he already had a house among the people with which he wanted to associate. Magic?

Nope. Star athletes and astronauts use visualization techniques to train for events and maneuvers in outer space. Visualization can be so impactful because the subconscious mind does not know whether you are actually running a race, or earning ten million dollars a film, or if you are just playing it out in your imagination. It has been proven scientifically that the same cells in the brain fire when you are sitting in a chair, eyes closed, imagining running a sprint in your mind as if you were really out on the track.

Such a powerful tool indeed, if it can work for the world's top athletes, astronauts and the super wealthy. I imagine that we all want to master this technique.

Jack Canfield suggests that we follow these three fun steps to better visualize for ourselves and strengthen that muscle in our minds for helping us manifest the life of our dreams.

Step 1) Imagine sitting in a movie theater, the lights dim, then the movie starts. It is a movie of you, doing whatever it is that you want to do better, perfectly. See it in as much detail as you are able, add in sights, sounds, smells and feelings that you would like to be experiencing as you engage in your activity.

Step 2) Get out of your chair (in your mind) walk up to the screen and enter into the movie. Now experience the whole thing again from inside of yourself, looking out through your eyes. This is called an 'Embodied Image' rather than a 'Distant Image.' It will deepen the impact of the experience, again we see everything in vivid detail, hear the sounds you would hear and feel the feelings you would feel.

Step 3) Finally walk back out of the screen that is still showing the picture of you performing perfectly, return to your seat in the theater, reach out, and grab the screen, shrink it to the size of a cracker, pop it in your mouth and swallow it. Imagine it becoming part of you on the cellular level, every cell of your body is lit up with a movie of you performing perfectly, like an appliance store where fifty televisions are all simultaneously tuned to a picture of you performing perfectly.

As stated above, this should be fun. Jack's exercise certainly leaves plenty of room for fun and creativity. As with everything else, this is just a suggestion to get you started, you must find what works best for you. This is where you should follow your feelings. If you are feeling frustrated, then you are not in the flow.

For myself, I like to visualize when I am out walking, I am relaxed, in nature and I have a few minutes to myself, I can get into the flow of thoughts and feelings, of having it now, whatever I choose to visualize. I have favorites, projects, and projections for my life, which I visualize often, with an almost giddy knowing that they are on their way. I do not feel impatient because I am able to see these things in all their glory and detail as if they are right in front of me any time I choose.

If I can do it, so can you. With practice and an open mind, a desire to improve your mental well being and hone your powerful skills of creation. You too can visualize the life of your dreams, in bold color, you can smell what that life smells like and feel the joy and happiness that you will feel as you bring it ever closer, day by day in your imagination first, then into your reality.

When you do, you will know how powerful you are and endeavor to create bigger, better visions for yourself, and the world in which we live. Let us join the ranks of our fellow visionaries and create a world where we can all manifest the life of our dreams.

LESSON #12

Meditation:

Calmness of Mind

∽

Buddha was asked, "What have you gained from meditation?" He replied, "Nothing, However, let me tell you what I have lost; anger, anxiety, depression, insecurity, fear of old age, and death."

Wise words from the Buddha about the importance of letting go, which is what meditation, at its core, is all about. The calming of the mind and spirit. A chance to slow down and separate our thoughts, to allow space for new thoughts to enter, that otherwise would not have had an opportunity to present themselves. Practicing meditation each day can improve the function of your brain with better attention, focus, stress management, impulse control, and self awareness.

As strange as it may sound, you can achieve all these things through a meditation practice, which when made a habit and efficiency is gained, the goal of 'nothing' will be achieved, as stated above, by the Buddha. The reason that 'nothingness' is so important is that the brain is the switching station between our physical being and the mind which is located outside of the body.

The brain on a typical day processes between 40,000 and 60,000 thoughts. Often these are the same 60,000 thoughts we experience day after day. What is commonly referred to as 'the Monkey Mind' because of the way it jumps around and chatters incessantly, is already chock full of activity, which leaves no room for new useful information or for peace of mind.

Meditation, in a nutshell, stripped down to its most basic function is a daily practice of 'giving your brain a breather.' Our brains function much better with a small break, even if it is just for a few minutes.

When you are able to hold an open space on the screen of your mind, even for a minute or two, you have just achieved something amazing. To slow and space your thoughts deliberately, we are taking back the control over our thoughts, we are now manning the switchboard and establishing a sense of mastery over our brain and bodies.

The brain is a powerful tool for us, the control center for our being. When no one is at the controls, our brains are left to run amok. Imagine the most powerful supercomputer in the world just left alone to do whatever it pleases. We have all heard of the movie series, 'The Terminator' in which our world becomes one of destruction and misery when the computers become 'self-aware' and take control. Similarly, on a perhaps slightly less dramatic level, our brains can cause all kinds of destruction in our lives if not steered in the right direction

As stated in many of these lessons, this is not meant to give you mastery over meditation or even to introduce you to all the different forms of meditation, as there are many and they differ greatly in their structures and practices. What may be helpful and feel right to one person may be down right torture to another.

Over the years I have learned about and attempted many different forms of meditation. None of them ever seemed to work the way that I thought they were supposed to, I would become discouraged, think that I just wasn't 'spiritual enough' or something of that nature and give up.

There are so many sources of information that stress the importance of a daily practice of meditation. Its benefits have been widely studied by science. MRI and brain scan technology verify what traditional eastern philosophy has told us for centuries about the brain.

From a technical standpoint, the whole brain is functionally, and structurally changed by deliberately slowing its thought functions on a daily basis. The different parts of the brain affected are as follows:

1. **Frontal Lobe**: This is the most highly evolved part of the brain, responsible for reasoning, planning, emotions, and self conscious awareness. During meditation, the frontal cortex goes offline.

2. **Parietal Lobe**: This part of the brain processes sensory information about the surrounding world, orienting you in time or space. During meditation, activity in the parietal lobe slows down.

3. **Thalamus**: The gatekeeper of the senses, this organ focuses your attention by funneling some sensory data deeper into the brain, and stopping other signals in their tracks. Meditation reduces the flow of incoming information to a trickle.

4. **Reticular Formation**: As the brain's sentry, this structure receives incoming stimuli and puts the brain on alert, ready to respond. Meditation dials back the arousal signal.

Now that we have some understanding of the effects and benefits of meditation, let's look at an approach to make the act of meditation as simple as possible so that we can all begin a daily practice in a relaxed and confident manner.

To start, we are going to sit for twenty minutes. I like to set a timer so that I don't have to worry about how long it's been or have to mentally keep track of time. Again, this is just to get us started, when efficiency and confidence are gained, the sky's the limit as to how long your meditations can be or what different styles to decide to practice. This is what works for me.

The timer is set for twenty minutes, the goal is to quiet the mind for two of those twenty minutes. We want to slow down our thoughts and create a gap between them, then hold that gap for as long as we can. This will take some practice. Just remember that twenty minutes of deliberate relaxation is the most precious gift you can give yourself, no matter what happens during that time. This is a winning situation, regardless of the outcome.

We have set the timer, during a time or in a space when we can be alone, uninterrupted by phone calls, spouses, dogs or kids. In a quiet, comfortable place, if possible, sit in 'the lotus' position, this is the posture most commonly associated with meditation. Legs crossed in front of you, hands resting on your knees, thumbs touching your index fingers to form a circle, back straight, eyes closed. This body posture helps to close your electrical currents in the body and allow that energy to flow in a loop. It also aligns your chakras and in my experience becomes a queue to your brain that it is time to meditate. If you are not able to sit like this, fear not, just do the best you are able to make yourself comfortable, though lying down is not recommended as you may just fall asleep.

Now that our timer is set, we are comfortable in our lotus position, eyes closed and we can begin to turn inwards and focus on our breathing. At first just notice it, become aware of it. Is it shallow, rapid, are you nervous? We want to take slow, deliberate, comfortable breaths. This is to tell our brains and our bodies that we are safe, and it is time to relax.

Once we have a good handle on our breathing and are feeling very relaxed, it is likely that you have begun to notice thoughts coming and going in your mind. You may see lights or flashing, hear voices or feel your attention being drawn elsewhere by sounds outside. Do not resist these things, instead acknowledge them and allow them to drift away.

You may experience a sense of numbness or weightlessness as you go deeper, just enjoy it. The space between that thought or distraction is what we are after. If you can hold that space without effort for a moment, let it be. If a thought comes along, acknowledge it and allow it on its way. Hold that space, without effort, continue on in this manner until the timer goes off. Open your eyes, feel the level of relaxation you have been able to achieve, sit with it for a moment, and enjoy it.

That's it, that is meditation in its simplest form. Certainly a powerful exercise even though you were physically doing very little. Meditation is unique among the other daily practices we have been learning about in that it can directly affect the brain in a physical manner.

While you were sitting there quietly, you were weakening the neural pathways that are deeply embedded, with regard to our fears, stories of pain and victimization, as it quiets the emotional centers associated with our reaction to events from the past or outside ourselves.

That gap that we held, provided us with an opportunity to look at these situations from a more practical, detached standpoint. Simultaneously, we strengthened the frontal areas of our brain which can, in turn, allow more positive emotions, longer lasting emotional stability, and heightened daily focus, along with more creativity, better memory, more compassion, and all this slows the aging process of the brain.

Meditation is a fascinating process, important to our spiritual awareness as well as our overall physical and emotional well being. This is truly a lesson that you can begin today and spend a lifetime mastering. The longer you practice this powerful exercise, the longer, and more pleasant that life is sure to be as you continue to manifest the life of your dreams.

LESSON #13

View All Experiences As a Blessing or a Lesson!

⁓

"A smooth sea never made for a skilled sailor."
—Franklin D Roosevelt

How often do we dwell upon the things we feel haven't gone our way?

How often do we reiterate the story of how things didn't go our way?

The stories that we tell others are the stories we tell ourselves. They are based on our perception of the experiences we have encountered. We use these stories to make sense of the situation, to justify them to ourselves, and others, to gain empathy or sympathy, when they hear of the tragedies bestowed upon us by a merciless universe. Situations beyond our control in which we had no choice but to endure the agony that lingers still today.

These are the stories that we tell ourselves, about ourselves and we share with others, to color their perception of us. We all have past traumas, we all have been treated unfairly at one time or another. We have all lost love, money or possessions. We have all known illness, injury or injustice. These things are inevitable in life.

Perhaps it was the sympathy bestowed upon us by well meaning parents that taught us to speak of our pains and traumas and hope that another would be able to 'kiss it better.' Perhaps it is the true effect of psychological and emotional trauma that so many of us have experienced because the people that raised us were themselves psychologically and emotionally damaged, raised by parents, and grandparents suffering from the same.

Whatever the cause of us, viewing ourselves as victims of life's circumstances, powerless to control them, and eager to share those stories with others to explain our lot in life. What if there was another way? A way totally different in its character, nature, and message.

> *"Every experience, no matter how bad it seems,*
> *holds within it a blessing of some kind. The goal is to find it."*
> —Buddha

One of the most transformational lessons in my life is this other way that I alluded to above. I was one of those people, a victim of circumstances beyond my control. Mistreated in my youth, bullied, victimized. I experienced heartbreak and deep grief over lost loved ones, of which I was not even consciously aware of for decades.

I have experienced psychological and emotional abuse on many levels throughout my life, often by those that I loved most. Hurt and abandoned by those people that I respected and thought were friends. This left me baffled for many years. Angry, broke, in debt, confused, unsure of myself, and where I stood, fearful of a future that held more of the same.

What had I done to deserve treatment like this? Why could I not get out ahead financially? How could I trust anyone new, let alone the people already in my life? I did know one thing for sure, I was not alone in feeling this way, it is a pervasive undercurrent in our society.

Once I discovered this all important lesson and practiced it in my life, a huge shift took place, now I want to share it with everyone that might need to hear this message just as I did. It could be you.

The message, once heard fully, understood and implemented will change the way you view your past, present and future. It did for me.

The simple concept of viewing each experience as a blessing and/or a lesson as often they are both, is the most transformational idea that I have ever encountered. We must perceive that each and every event, circumstance, person, or situation was presented to us for our own highest good.

Now, this may be a huge pill to swallow. I agree that at first there will be some argument and rebuttal, but stick with me. It can be very challenging to swing your point of view around and consider some of our worst tragedies as gifts given to us by God, as part of the infinite plan.

Think of it like this: If we are all pieces of God, divine expressions of our ever expanding universe, endowed with talents and gifts unmatched by any previous soul upon this earth. If we, as beings of light and consciousness have come here to this plane of physical existence to indeed expand and explore all aspects of the divine, to find out, in fact, is it true?

Then would we not, as scientists do, need tests and experiments to root out our true nature and essence? We must then view each and every experience in our lives, without judgement, as a blessing and/or a lesson as often they are both, intertwined to bring us emotional wisdom and knowledge born of those experiences— so that each of those experiences, situations, people, and circumstances were set forth to develop us into the people whom we have become, today, so that we can advance to be the people that the world will need us to be tomorrow. Truly, each and every one of us, has a place at this table we call creation. Now more than ever we need to draw upon the collective wisdom that life has bestowed upon us.

To view each experience as a blessing and/or a lesson brings forth that wisdom. No longer will you view those past trauma's as unjust or unfair, instead you will see them as tests of strength and will. The grief of that loss is a gift given to you, meant to be passed along to others that need it in the form of empathy. One cannot know empathy without loss.

That lack of financial gain you experienced, that was the gift of humbleness, to show us that effort does not equal economy, and that money does not dictate one's value. That heartbreak was a gift of contrast, it was actually a gift of love, for how can one truly know love without its absence and once it is found, we now know how important it is to maintain it as to not hurt another, through those experiences.

When we change our perceptions about our own experiences and redefine what they meant to us, we begin to view the people and events around us in a whole new light. Those experiences that affected you most deeply, those are now your strengths. Gifts given to you to share with others. If you were severely mistreated, that was a gift of contrast given to you so that you will know that feeling, experientially and not mistreat others.

If you were beaten or abused physically, a common and far too prevalent cause of continued violence, often by victims of violence themselves. If you view that violence upon you as a gift of contrast, see the lesson that violence solves nothing, then the blessing can be one of gentleness, kindness, nurturing, and courage, that you can then share, to help others move beyond what has weakened them and show them that source of strength—the gift with which they have now been bestowed.

I am sure you can see clearly now how viewing each experience as a blessing and/or a lesson can be so transformational and empowering. You are no longer a victim of circumstance, you are a receiver of experiential wisdom with a responsibility to share that gift with the world around you, empowering others to see the value of their life experiences, and all that they have to offer. Expand upon this idea and you will see that not only does this change our view of the world, but it also changes the world's view of us.

We now become leaders, advocates, teachers, healers, and conscious creators. We become the people that we have always dreamed of being, we truly are the ones that the world has been waiting for, it's time for us to wake up and see our value in this world and to share it wherever we are able. Those past experiences are our initiation, our education, they are our strength when strength is needed, they are the wisdom that guides us, they are our gentle nature, when kindness is due. They are our empathy, when others are in pain and the healing that you now share for yourself and others.

Indeed all of our experiences have been a blessing and/or a lesson leading us to be who we are today so that we can be the people of love, light, and strength that the world will need us to be tomorrow as we collectively manifest the life of our dreams. Bless us all.

LESSON #14

Happiness:

It's a Decision, Not a Destination

Life, Liberty, and the pursuit of Happiness. These are the three unalienable rights that our forefathers perceived to be above all else in our Declaration of Independence. What is Happiness?

According to Wikipedia, the term happiness is used in the context of mental or emotional states including positive or pleasant emotions ranging from contentment to intense joy. It is also used to describe satisfaction, flourishing, and subjective well being.

OK, What is happiness not?

Happiness is not, feeling good all the time, feeling good all the time can be induced by drugs, and drugs do not equate happiness.

So, now we have some idea of what happiness is and what it is not, but that doesn't really feel like enough, does it?

Happiness is different things to different people, a truly deep philosophical and emotional subject.

"Happiness is when what you think,
what you say and what you do are in harmony."
—Mahatma Gandhi

In my search for the meaning of happiness, I found many different ways to categorize and explain the experience of happiness. Overall, happiness is best described as an even keeled mood that is mentally healthier than a mood in which you experience great heights of elation regularly. One could take that to mean that to be happy is more an underlying theme for life rather than on a mountain of euphoria or wildly joy filled all the time.

To help us better understand different levels of happiness, Benjamin Radcliff: PhD, in his article published in psychology today: *The economy of Happiness.* Describes the three levels of happiness

Level one: The balance between our transient emotions both positive (joy) and negative (anxiety).

Level two: Our cognitive self judgements about our life in general, long term sense (perspective).

Level three: A focus on flourishing and finding meaning in life.

The first level refers to one's current emotional state. If we could measure a person's emotional state over time, then we could gauge or calculate their overall emotional state, this provides an objective happiness measure with all other things being equal, kind of like a happiness score.

The second Level of happiness differs in that it objects to the idea that happiness is a mathematical score that you add up the good experiences and the bad experiences, weighted by how good or bad they are.

It also draws our attention to happiness, not as a series of moments but as a stable orientation in one's life, as if it were part of their personality, more readily allowing one to define happiness for themselves rather than reducing it to someone else's judgement that happiness is about seeking pleasure and avoiding emotional pain.

The Third level of happiness refers to a life or lifestyle that is in 'flow,' which is characterized as the mental state in which we are positively and fully engrossed in some pleasurable activity such that our sense of self disappears. This is very similar to eastern Philosophy, along the lines of enlightenment, which is achieved when one learns to be free of the "Self"

A thorough if not somewhat ambiguous answer to the question. I am still wondering, What is Happiness?

According to Happify Daily, what's happiness anyway? By Dr Acacia Parks PhD. You will not necessarily " arrive" at happiness. It takes regular effort to maintain happiness. Some established techniques for feeling happier are keeping a gratitude journal, meditation, exercise, music, art, healthy diet, hobbies, pets, and clubs are habits and activities, not just one shot events.

> *"There is no way to happiness, happiness is the way!"*
> —Thich Nhat Hanh

I believe that a person could research and study happiness extensively, as there are many opinions and tons of information out there. What I think it really comes down to is this. Happiness can be achieved each and every moment of every day with one simple concept. To give of yourself to another. To hold in your mind, if even for a moment, a kind thought towards another is a start. To give back to your community. To give to your partner or spouse. To give a special gift to a family member or coworker, it needn't be expensive, just from the heart. Children know how to give freely of themselves, many of us have forgotten how.

Have you ever spontaneously given a person in need the assistance they required at the moment? Given a homeless person a meal or a few dollars?

Have you ever picked up a hitchhiker and found out that you saved their day? How about visiting a friend at the hospital and bringing them flowers or a scratch off lottery ticket, baking some cookies for a neighbor just so you had a reason to stop by and say, "hello?"

Giving is the way to daily happiness. The more ways you can give of yourself, the happier you can be. The act of giving is contagious and so is 'the happiness.' A person that receives a gift is much more likely to give to someone else, and on and on it goes, the ripple effect. Just like a stone cast into a pond the feeling of happiness and giving radiates outward.

We have all been touched by stories of giving, nothing warms the heart quite like a tale of selflessness. The 'pay it forward' movement is just such a story. I am sure everyone has experienced a pay it forward moment, popularized by the 2000 film titled: 'Pay it Forward,' where a struggling mother, a social studies teacher whose placid life is in perfect order and the student whose class assignment has profound repercussions when, instead of paying it back, the recipient of kindness must pay it forward.

The assignment is simple. 1) look at the world around you and fix what you don't like 2) something that they can't do for themselves 3) Do it for them and they do it for 3 other people. Teacher Eugene Simonet never expects one of his students to take the assignment to heart, much less the profound, unanticipated effects that Trevor McKinney's actions will have on the world. A must see if you have not already, one small act of kindness CAN change the world.

One could wonder why giving feels so good and again we return to science to help us understand. Humans are social animals. We are wired to help each other. Neuroscience has demonstrated that giving is a powerful pathway for creating more personal joy and improving overall health.

The Neurochemicals of Happiness, also known as the Happiness Trifecta are Dopamine, Serotonin and Oxytocin. Any activity that boosts the production of these three neurochemicals will cause a boost in mood.

The benefits of releasing these three, powerful chemicals in the brain go on and on.

Dopamine is connected to motivation and arousal.

Serotonin is a regulator of sleep, digestion, memory, learning and appetite.

Oxytocin, also known as 'the Cuddle Hormone' is among the most ancient of our neurochemicals and has a powerful effect on the brain and the body. When Oxytocin flows, blood pressure decreases and the foundation for sexual arousal is built. Bonding increases, social fears are reduced along with trust and empathy being enhanced. Oxytocin is also an anti-inflammatory while reducing pain and wound healing.

So, if giving allows us to secrete all the chemicals at once. We owe it to ourselves to give as often as possible.

Helping others can take many forms, small repeated bursts of the 'Happiness Trifecta' will produce the most benefit so find ways to give and give often. All giving works wonders, no matter how small an act may seem to you. Holding a door for a stranger, smiling at a child looking up at you, listening to a friend that needs to 'talk things out.' Sure, you can donate to charity, raise money, work in a food pantry, the list is endless.

Bottom line, you should fill every day with small acts of giving, random acts of kindness, even if it is only a smile and a kind word. Gifts like that can have a huge impact on both you and the world around you, so give freely, give often and bask in the mental and physical effects of your actions. Every time you do, you are making a decision to be happy and to share that happiness with the world around you. You might end up making our world a better place, one random act of kindness at a time. Who knows what impact it will have on the world around us as we manifest not only the life of our dreams, but share little bits of that dream with those around us.

LESSON #15

Excitement and Nervousness Are The Same Emotion

❧

*"Stop worrying about what can go wrong and
get excited about what can go right."*
—kushandwizdom

What is it that separates top performers from the rest of us? It may be something much simpler than you think. The answer: whether it be athletes, business leaders, actors, and anyone else that is seemingly excelling at whatever it is they are doing is a difference in how they perceive a particular emotion.

That emotion has two names, just like a coin has two sides, so does this feeling, and we all get it. The positive side is called excitement and the negative side is called nervousness or anxiety. I prefer to stick with the term nervousness as I believe that anxiety has a chronic stigma attached, where nervousness is more a feeling in the moment, energetically.

How often have you heard an interview with a high performing athlete, let's say for example, the olympics. You have athletes from all over the world, every age, gender, race and sport. When asked either before or after their event how they are feeling, they will tell you almost unanimously:

"I am excited to be here," that's it. That's the trick, the difference. You do not ever hear them say: "I am nervous." Why?

Well, first of all we must understand that these high functioning people did not just get off their couch one day and show up to the Olympics or that Broadway play or whatever it is they are doing. These folks have been coached and trained to win, period. Not a single one of our Olympic athletes spends years in training to travel to wherever the games are, to lose. That goes for musical performers, professional athletes, top corporate business leaders, politicians and public speakers.

Understand that these folks may be experiencing the butterflies in their stomach, the dry mouth, sweaty palms and a heartbeat that they are sure is visible through their jacket. What most of us might perceive as signs of nervousness, for that you would be right.

Except that in perceiving these keyed up emotions as nervousness suggests that where some kind of uncertainty lies ahead, there is self doubt or a fear of the uncertainty. Instead of fighting, the mind is considering flight, looking for the exits, trying to find a safe place to hide away from these sensations. This is the emotional state where we shy away from challenges and fear trying something new, venturing into unknown territory, where we are unable to know for certain what is to be gained.

As the saying goes: "Nothing ventured, nothing gained."

So that feeling of nervousness holds the unaware, the uncoached, the untrained in our safe havens of the mind.

Our top performers on the other hand have been coached and trained for countless hours to perceive that feeling as excitement about what lies ahead, a chance to pit themselves, their honed skills and talents against another, an opportunity to compete, to win. That feeling of excitement is their edge. All of their senses are heightened, the blood and the adrenaline are coursing through their veins. In their minds, they are ready for anything that is thrown at them. These are the men and women that will walk off the battlefield because they believe they can, carrying those that doubted they had what it took. Sadly, those emotions were one and the same.

The technical term is Anxiety Reappraisal, which is fairly self explanatory and describes what is going on quite succinctly. We could also view it in terms of:

Threat mindset: Self doubt and fear creep in about the uncertainty of the situation, causing us to alleviate ourselves of the physical sensation we are feeling, and the visual images of failure we are creating in our minds.

Or

Opportunity mindset: Where the feelings of heightened awareness and energy coupled with positive self-talk and self assuredness that you are ready, and able to overcome the uncertainty that lies ahead are expressed outwardly.

It is as simple as that. How we talk to ourselves is how we talk to others about ourselves. When we are stepping outside our comfort zone, no matter what it is and that feeling arises, flip that script and realize that you are excited, you can handle any task that lays ahead, you can thrive in the uncertainty and you will celebrate the victory of that occasion.

Repeat after me: I am not nervous, I am excited, I am not nervous, I am excited. I am excited to be here, I am excited to meet you, I am excited to be a part of this. I too am excited and know that I am also excited for you as you manifest the life of your dreams.

LESSON #16

Fear and Anger are Kissing Cousins

❦

"Fear is the path to the dark side. Fear leads to anger,
anger leads to hate, hate leads to suffering."
—George Lucas

The reason I titled this lesson 'fear and anger are kissing cousins' is because I wanted to make it a memorable one. We have all known those two cousins that were just a bit too close and nothing but trouble, where one is to be found, the other is surely nearby, so are fear and anger.

Fear is characterized by an unpleasant feeling triggered by the perception of danger, real or imagined.

Anger is characterized by antagonism toward someone or something you feel has deliberately done you wrong.

One of the most profound truths that I discovered for myself during the early stages of my personal development was that when anger showed up, I should be looking for the underlying fear. Which was a real relief for me, before that realization, I would become angry in situations where I did not even understand why I was angry.

Which can be both confusing and embarrassing when you are unable to explain an angry outburst or to even understand the cause of it. Being unaware of the relationship between these two emotions is quite commonplace, especially for men in our western society. We are taught to bury our emotions, especially fear, to not show signs of weakness. Sadly, it seems to be somewhat acceptable to express anger. We see violence on TV and movies, where angry men with martial arts skills and guns make the world a better place by wiping out the bad guys that are creating fear.

That works for TV but in today's society, unbridled anger has no place and it certainly does not properly resolve problems.

Fear and anger physiologically are very similar, with virtually the same effect on the autonomic nervous system with respect to cardiovascular, respiratory and the outward appearance of the skin, such as redness and sweating.

Similar physiology that is part of one emotion can naturally lead into another when triggered by an appropriate stimulus. If you realize that someone has made you afraid of them and is therefore responsible for your negative feelings, then you may feel angry towards them for thwarting your goal of feeling good about your life. I have found this to be a recurring experience for me, and I feel compelled to share it.

This is where awareness and personal responsibility come into play. As I personally discovered, much to my relief, as I became more self-aware, as stated above, having uncontrolled angry outbursts or just feeling angry without being able to explain why is both confusing and embarrassing. It feels this way because you are not in control of your emotions, nor do you understand why. Explaining or articulating your feelings to another, be it your boss, friend, spouse, or children, then presents a real challenge because you don't know what is causing the anger.

As I became more aware of myself, observing, and questioning my own thoughts, feelings, and behaviors. I began to see a pattern; when I had a thought that scared me, I began to feel angry. Often then, when I would feel the anger rise up, then I would feel guilty for not having a better handle on myself. Observing this pattern allowed me to uncover a hidden truth about myself and my emotions.

The truth was that anger was an acceptable mask for fear. When anger showed up, it was to hide an underlying fear. This was a revelation for me, one that I have shared with many people who also struggle with anger, both men and women. Having a new awareness that this is what is really going on internally is not always enough to stop from getting angry, but that awareness and growing emotional intelligence can allow you to react more quickly. I would like to illustrate with an example from my own life around the time when I first started to become aware of the relationship between fear and anger in myself.

It was a beautiful summer day and we decided to grill hotdogs for lunch. I suddenly realized that we didn't have any buns in the cupboard, there is a little store about a mile down the road, we live out in a fairly rural area, so I hopped in my car and quickly headed off to the store for buns. At this time, we had a young energetic dog, named Ryder, that had only been living with us for a short time.

As I looked in the rearview, pulling up to the stop sign, not far from our house, I could see Ryder running enthusiastically behind my car. At this point, it had been less than three months since we had lost a beloved dog to a motorist on an adjacent road, in which the dog was mysteriously struck and killed in the early morning hours when we let her out to relieve herself, the driver didn't stop, we were left with many questions. So, when I looked back to see Ryder running down the road, I was stricken with fear.

How did I respond? With an outburst of anger that would scare the crap out of just about everyone around. My children were upstairs in the house witnessing me screaming at the top of my lungs to the dog, pointing towards the house, barking demands at the dog, swearing, stomping and putting on an angry display. Something I am not proud of, needless to say, the dog's enthusiasm was gone, as he scuttled back to the house, tail between his legs. My partner looked terrified as well. I got back in the car and proceeded to the store.

Immediately I questioned my reaction, whereas before I may have just felt guilty for a few days about my lack of control. I asked myself "What was that all about?" The answer came back as fear, plain and simple, fear. Fear of this dog thinking it was okay to chase cars, fear of my family having to experience that again, fear that I may be the cause of that happening again. All of those fears became apparent to me as I drove.

When I got home, I explained to my partner Joni and the children why I had reacted that way. I told them about my fear and they expressed theirs. I apologized to them for overreacting, I hugged the dog and apologized to him too. He wasn't bad, just young and inexperienced, my reaction wasn't fair to him. I wasn't some horrible monster, I was afraid, scared that someone I loved would be injured or be in danger. I was afraid for everyone at that moment.

This was a great relief. Self-awareness and personal responsibility took this situation and turned it into a bonding moment for us all—a teaching moment for myself and my children. I was able to explain to my two boys then, that if I am angry; I am really scared, and that it is okay to be afraid. I learned something about myself that day and so did everyone else.

I hope that my story has illustrated why fear and anger are kissing cousins. They are related and where you find one, the other is sure to be nearby. Allow this awareness to serve you. Allow it to help you and your family become more aware of what is really happening. In our culture, especially men but I have met women also, that do not know how to properly express emotions. Emotional intelligence comes from self awareness and personal responsibility. Let's learn together and grow on the premise that all emotion has its place, that it is okay to express fear, it is not a sign of weakness that needs to be covered up.

So much of the violence in our society can likely be attributed to fear. Let's take a moment and envision a world where all this violence no longer exists and that all people are able to express themselves appropriately without acting out. I for one think that sounds like a beautiful dream, where emotional intelligence for every man, woman and child is encouraged and supported. I am holding that vision for our world, walking in the direction of it becoming a reality, and spreading awareness along the way. Join me and let's make this world a healthy emotional place for us all as we collectively manifest the life of our dreams.

LESSON #17

Love vs. Fear

∽

I believe that John Lennon said it all in the following quote: "There are two basic motivating forces, fear and love, when we are afraid, we pull back from life. When we are in love, we open to all that life has to offer with passion, excitement and acceptance. We need to learn to love ourselves first, in all our glory and imperfections. If we cannot love ourselves, we cannot fully open to our ability to love others or our potential to create. Evolution and all hopes for a better world rest in the fearlessness and open hearted vision of people who embrace life."

Wise words indeed, such a shame that Mr. Lennon was taken from this world so soon. Can you imagine forty more years of wisdom like that being shared in our world? It could be a whole different place. John Lennon was certainly, during his life and career, an advocate for love. Sadly it was fear that caused his untimely death on December 8th, 1980 at the hands of Mark David Chapman.

Chapman's statement to police was that he was angry about Lennon's lifestyle and public statements, such as his statement that "the Beatles are more popular than Jesus." As we have just learned in the previous lesson, anger is often a mask for fear. Mark David Chapman's fear led to his anger, which expressed itself in the public murder of a man that spread a message of love to the world.

Fear is the word we use to describe our emotional reaction to something that seems dangerous, but the word 'fear' is used in another way also, to name something of which a person often feels afraid. People fear things or situations that make them feel unsafe or unsure.

Love encompasses a range of strong and positive emotional and mental states, from the most sublime virtue or good habit, the deepest interpersonal affection to the simplest pleasure.

According to the triangular theory of love, developed by Psychologist Robert Sternberg, the three components of love are: intimacy, passion and commitment. Intimacy encompasses feelings of attachment, closeness, connectedness, and bondedness. Passion encompasses drives connected to romantic attraction and reciprocation of that attraction. Commitment comes in to tie the two together, it is a decision for two people sharing these love components with each other, and planning for the future.

Love and fear are two root emotions.

Jealousy, anger, dismay, loneliness, grief, shame, guilt, frustration, doubt and insecurity are all fear based emotions. Fear is about being separated from one another, fear based emotions seek to separate you from me and us from them over there. Fear is the cause for violence and suffering in the world. Fear is the cause of racism, poverty, murder, and politics. Our world in many ways is a fear based world, a world of lack and limitation, enforced with laws and punishment.

On the other hand, Love based emotions include: hope, joy, gratitude, peace, faith, trust, confidence, happiness, connection, forgiveness, openness, passion, freedom, harmony, honesty, beauty, compassion, self-love, self appreciation, respect, acceptance, and understanding.

Imagine if our world was structured around emotions like that. Those are powerfully positive emotions. With a world based on those emotions, every person could thrive, there would be enough to go around. No one living in a state of love that deep would allow another to suffer.

Our world is a complex place, certainly there is room for both emotions, just as there is room for day and night, yin and yang and all the other dichotomies that make this world a balanced place. It is perfectly natural for a person to know the feelings of fear, but choose to respond with love. Fear has its place in keeping us safe if we are alone in a jungle full of hungry beasts, a far cry from our highly structured society.

In choosing an emotion to be the undercurrent of your life and your reality, I would hope that more and more of us that are becoming self and spiritually aware, that are taking more personal responsibility for our thoughts and behavior will choose love. Fear has caused enough destruction in this world. Wars, politics, big business, pollution, global warming, the list goes on.

Let us, the stewards of this earth, let us choose love. Let us live our lives with thoughtfulness, kindness and integrity. Let us raise our awareness and the awareness of those around us, to embrace love and allow fear to slip back into the shadows where it belongs. Embracing love towards our fellow humans, our earth and the inhabitants that share this reality with us, is the single most God like thing we can do. After all we are expressions of the expansive nature of universal intelligence.

"If you knew who walked beside you at all times, on the path that you have chosen, you could never experience fear or doubt again."
—Wayne Dyer

Let us choose love and collectively create a world that we can all be proud of, in the age old battle between love vs fear, I am rooting for love. Who is with me? It can be the only true path to manifesting the life of your dreams.

LESSON #18

Success vs. Failure

∽

"Failure is simply the opportunity to begin again,
this time more intelligently."
—Henry Ford

Success and failure are often intertwined as we move through life. How many times throughout history has what appeared at first to be a massive failure, turned out to be a resounding success? The opposite is also true. Let us explore the true meanings and value of both success and failure so we can appreciate the important roles that each of them play for us along our journey.

Let's begin by discussing failure. Failure is an emotional response rather than a set destination. Thomas Edison attempted approximately 10,000 variations of materials for the filament of his light bulb, that has always astounded me. At any one point he could have thrown in the towel and been a failure, instead he endured and invented one of the most useful things that the human race has created next to the wheel. This is a prime example of success vs failure, it is a habit of mind. There is some great information in Maxwell Maltz's book: *Psycho Cybernetics*. I would like to share a few ideas so we can more fully understand failure and success.

The failure type personality has its symptoms, we need to be able to recognize these failure symptoms in ourselves so we can do something about them. No one is immune to these negative feelings and attitudes, even the most successful personalities experience them at times. The important thing is to recognize them for what they are and take positive action to course correct. The negative feedback signals, so that they can be recognized, according to Maxwell Maltz. The negative feedback signals to watch for are; frustration, hopelessness, futility, aggressiveness, insecurity, loneliness, uncertainty, resentment and emptiness.

No one sits down and deliberately decides to develop these traits, they don't just happen either, nor are they an indication of the imperfection of human nature. Each of these negatives was originally adopted as a way to solve a difficulty or problem. We adopt them because we mistakenly see them as a way out of some difficulty. They have meaning and purpose, although based on a mistaken premise.

I can affirm from personal experience that what Mr. Maltz is telling us about failure is true. His lesson struck a chord with me about the negative feedback mechanism of failure. One which I had been using my whole life under a false premise.

For me, it was that I needed to present myself as a failure or fail on certain fundamental levels so that I would not make others in my life feel inferior. It is not hard to see what a twisted logic this is, and a detrimental one at that.

A great deal of soul searching, awareness and personal responsibility went into shifting those thoughts of failure and eradicating them from my mind. I even found that my failure mindset contained within it a fear of success. The two were intertwined and kept me in a state of lack. If this resonates with you, I encourage you to learn more on the subject and find a way to shift that mindset as it is not serving you or the people that helped initiate it. I will conclude our lesson of failure with this quote.

"We learn wisdom from failure much more than from success, we often discover what we will do by finding out what we will not do, and probably he who never made a mistake, never made a discovery."
—Samuel Smiles

Moving on to the other side of the coin is the term 'success,' it has nothing to do with prestige symbols, but with creative accomplishment. Rightly speaking, no one should attempt to be 'a success' but everyone should attempt to be successful. Trying to be a success in terms of acquiring prestige symbols and wearing certain badges leads to neuroticism, frustration and unhappiness.

The Noah Webster dictionary defines success as 'The satisfactory accomplishment of a goal sought after.' Creative striving for a goal that is important to you as a result of your own deep felt needs, aspirations, and talents brings happiness as well as success because you will be functioning as you were meant to function. Human's by nature are goal striving beings and because we are built this way, we are not happy unless we are functioning as we are made to function, as a goal striver. Thus true success and true happiness not only go together but enhance each other.

I too once had a warped picture of success, as I am sure many of us do. The fact is as stated by Mr. Maltz, that success is about creatively striving for goals that meet our deep down needs. That is sure to be different for each and every one of us. Success is not a Lamborghini in the garage for all of us. Success could be selling your hand spun pottery online and donating the proceeds to a children's charity. That could make you feel like the most successful person on the planet. If it does, then you are. One of the ways that we can ensure our success in the future is to look back at the ways that we have already been successful.

This exercise was a real eye opener for me so I want to share it with you. Simply take a piece of paper and write the numbers 1-100 in several columns, this may require a few sheets. Then next, to each number write a success that you have accomplished in your life. I will help you out by telling you what to write for number one. At birth, you succeeded in coming into this world, seeing as how the infant mortality rate is somewhere between 34 and 49 percent worldwide, depending on the source. So you were a success just coming into this world, from there, the sky's the limit, unless you are Elon Musk, who doesn't even want to be limited by the sky. List all of your successes, have fun with it and soon you will realize; every step in your life held some measure of success. Give it a shot, write down graduations, great test scores, your driver's license, family, children and on and on, really get into it. When you hit 100, write 101-200, and keep it going. If you run out of successes to write down and still have numbers on the page, consider it to be like one to grow on. For your future successes, plan them out and write them down with due dates, then get working on them.

Success is a mindset, in order to achieve that mindset, you must be open to success and see it in every aspect of your life. Consider this often, here I will leave you with one last thought on success; remember to make it fun and do it with love as you manifest the life of your dreams.

"People rarely succeed unless
they have fun in what they are doing."
—Dale Carnegie

LESSON #19

Make The Decision

In considering how to begin this lesson about decision, I have the lyrics from a song performed by the Canadian band 'Rush' ringing in my head. From the 1980 album, 'Permanent Waves' is a track called 'Freewill' which got a lot of airplay on a local radio station over the years, so this is a song I have heard maybe thousands of times in my life, it never failed to catch my attention.

> There are those who think life
>
> Has nothing left to chance
>
> A host of holy horrors
>
> To direct our aimless dance
>
> A planet of playthings
>
> We dance on strings
>
> Of powers we cannot perceive
>
> The stars aren't aligned
>
> Or the Gods are malign
>
> Blame is better to give than receive

You can choose a ready guide

In some celestial voice

If you choose not to decide

You still have made a choice

It is those last two lines that over the years have struck a chord with me. "If you choose not to decide, you still have made a choice."

How many of us have experienced life by default? Not truly making a decision out of fear or ignorance. How many of us have felt that we had no choice in the path that our lives have taken. I am willing to bet that if we are all honest with ourselves and willing to be honest with others, that a large segment of the population would admit that they are living lives with circumstances that they would not have chosen, had they known that they were making a choice.

It stands to reason that before an action is to be taken, no matter what it is that a decision of some sort must be made. How many people struggle with indecision, the most common reason of all for being indecisive is fear of failure, by making a decision you might be wrong and nobody likes to be wrong.

Indecisiveness is defined as a maladaptive trait resulting in difficulty making decisions, across time, and situations. Indecision is positively correlated with measures of anxiety, worry, and depression.

I can attest to the frustration of living in fear of making the wrong decision, to the point where many times you feel paralyzed and unable to choose. I can recall that feeling where my brain would just seize up. I am sure that I am not alone in this experience. It can be quite a debilitating situation, especially if you have a family, children or an important role in business where others are looking to you to make an important decision.

Even a simple one, like what color to paint the living room can put some into a tailspin, it can be embarrassing to not be able to choose confidently. Certainly as time goes on, this can become a recurring issue in your life and lead to poor self esteem and hopelessness, hence the reason that indecisiveness is a symptom linked with major depressive disorders.

"Nothing happens until you decide.
Make a decision and watch your life move forward."
—Oprah Winfrey

I can remember a time in my life. my marriage had long been in trouble, we were seeing a marriage counselor and I was doing my one on one with the counselor. She listened for a while as I rattled on about all the implications of where my marriage was heading, then informed me that I needed to make a decision. I remember looking at her for a moment, feeling horrified, paralyzed. She told me that I needed to stop worrying about everyone else, my wife, my children especially, and make a decision because no one else was going to do it and it needed to be done.

I was infuriated, I was so upset that I was going to have to make a decision that would negatively impact my family, or so I perceived, basically in order to save myself. I was being treated disrespectfully by my spouse and it had been going on for a long time. It was very clear to anyone even slightly aware of our relationship, that something needed to change.

Surely, the children were being adversely affected by the unresolvable toxicity between us. We had already tried to 'talk it out' for well over a year, so the counselor was right. It was time to make a decision, because without a decision, one cannot take definitive action. I believe it was the next day that I came to terms with the decision I had to make. I saw the toll that years of emotional abuse had taken on my life and the results of that on our family. For the first time, in many years, I put myself and my wellbeing as a priority and made a decision.

A month later I found myself sitting down with an attorney, signing papers necessary to begin the divorce process. It was the hardest decision I had ever made. I felt sick turning against my wife, possibly hurting the children in the process. From that moment on, I knew my life and the lives of my family members would be forever changed.

Even though I felt ill with fear and guilt, I had for the first time a glimmer of hope that things were going to change and change they did. I am so happy and grateful that I made that decision, it has not always been easy, but it sure has been worth it. All the pain was worth my freedom, my emotional health, it has created a tighter bond with my children, one that I likely could not have experienced previously and showed me that my wellbeing is a priority.

I tell you my story to illustrate that once the decision is made, do not look back, do not second guess your decision, no matter how challenging it may seem. It takes a level of self love, dedication and determination to live the life of your dreams. We must look within, look at every area of your life and ask these questions. Am I on course? Am I growing, mentally, emotionally and spiritually? If there is anything that is preventing you from living your greatest life, make the tough decision to let it go.

Indecision can be mentally and emotionally exhausting. As with so many of our other mental faculties that we discussed, decision making is very much a skill that with practice will come more easily. Often there is not sufficient data available to enable one to see all the implications of a decision, making it a challenge to know what is the correct decision to make. This is where it is important to bring your values into play. Aligning with core personal values can simplify the decision making process.

The process for discerning core personal values is a relatively simple exercise and can be a real eye opener. It is important to become aware of your personal core values, if you are not already, so that they may assist you in the decision making process. Once you have established your core values, it will be much more efficient to make yes and no decisions, as it will be clear whether these decisions align with your values.

Here are three simple steps to help you discover your core values:

1. Take a look at the core values listed below. Choose no less than 3 and no more than 5 values that seem important to you.

2. Define for yourself, in writing, what each of those 3-5 values means to you. This will help you make the necessary yes and no decisions.

3. Run the 3-5 core values that you have selected through the litmus test of the following questions to determine if they are in fact core values.

A. Would you honestly sacrifice any of your core values for money?

B. Have you lost any core values in times of stress?

C. Do you hold any doubt that this core value will still hold true many years in the future?

D. Would you stop holding these values if at some point they put you at a competitive disadvantage?

If you answered yes to any of these questions then it is not a core value and requires re-evaluation.

If you answered no to the questions then it is a core value of your essence.

List of core values:

Authenticity	Freedom	Loyalty
Achievement	Faith	Meaningful Work
Adventure	Fame	Openness
Authority	Friendship	Peace
Autonomy	Fun	Pleasure
Balance	Growth	Passion
Beauty	Happiness	Popularity

Boldness	Honesty	Recognition
Compassion	Humor	Religion
Challenge	Influence	Reputation
Citizenship	Inner-harmony	Respect
Community	Justice	Responsibility
Competency	Kindness	Security
Contribution	Knowledge	Self-respect
Creativity	Leadership	Success
Curiosity	Learning	Spirituality
Determination	Love	Stability
Wealth	Wisdom	

Over time, humans have developed four ways of making decisions: instincts, subconscious beliefs, conscious beliefs, and core values. It is fairly normal in this day and age for people to use the first three methods of decision making. From an evolutionary standpoint, core value based decisions are relatively new, but are becoming more prevalent as we collectively evolve to higher levels of consciousness.

Value based decisions are necessary for individual and self actualization. Values allow us to transcend belief, the structures of our parental and social conditioning, so that we become more fully aware of who we are and can live more authentically. Additionally, values help us to transcend our cultural/ ethic's beliefs by uniting us around shared basic human principles. With value based decisions, people can work out for themselves what they need to do, should do and conversely not do, as to become responsible and accountable for their actions.

Now that we can see how making a decision and following through with it can empower the change and direction that we are looking to achieve in our lives. Indecision loses its grip on us, no longer do we have to be held back with trepidation when our next move is in question. Once we have established and accepted our core personal values, the decisions about our path laid before us become all too easy.

We can now live authentically as we know who we are and where we want to go. I know that from personal experience the power of making decisions confidently and the assurance of knowing what my core values are, guiding me in each situation I encounter. I hope that you, too, soon will be feeling empowered along your path. Let us go boldly into the future and never look back as we manifest the life of our dreams.

LESSON #20

It's All About You

‿◦‿

"Only the truth of who you are, if realized, will set you free."
—Eckhart Tolle

It is all about you. All of these lessons are about you. Personal development is all about you. We cannot control others. We cannot change our family members. We cannot dictate to our communities how they should be running. We cannot influence others on the internet, no matter how hard we try. What we can do is work on ourselves. Change ourselves, open up to new habits and ideas. We can learn, grow, and choose a new perspective. We can choose to respect others and their differences. Ultimately, we get to choose who we are and what we bring to this life, and to some degree, what we get out of it.

Personal development in all its various forms leads us down the path to find our authenticity. The authentic self that we seek is the self that prioritizes living by our values, pursuing our purpose and fighting for causes that we care about. For most of us, the authentic-self is buried deep in the subconscious mind, where it remains hard to identify and let out.

Have you ever felt deep down that something was missing in your life, as if you had a different calling, were destined for something different than the track you are currently on? This may be the longing of the authentic-self, the self that would have emerged before social conditioning set in at the early stages of life.

We are all born geniuses, gifted and beautiful in our own right. As we grow and begin to integrate into our family structures, into our schools, and eventually become a part of our community, we all look to fit in, and often, when we do, we give up aspects of our authentic-self.

What we adopt to fit into social situations and our society as a whole is called the adaptive self, which is just what it sounds like, it is the version of ourselves that adapts to our environment and social stimuli. Starting in childhood, gaining momentum through our adolescent phases and continuing into adulthood. Our adaptive self, shapes and molds to the conditions at hand as we move through life. The notion that we are the same person for our entire lives is a ridiculous one indeed. We are all changing and growing throughout our lives, according to the situations and conditions encountered. These are the things that shape us, especially if we are living somewhat unconsciously, not responding to life in line with our core values, but rather living in a reactive manner to whatever pops up in front of us, so we develop the adaptive self.

The self that we seek is the authentic-self. First, though, we must figure out where we are. We must begin by observing our adaptive self. What does it believe? How does it react under pressure? How does it respond to challenges? Take time to notice whether those responses feel authentic or not. By identifying which responses feel authentic and which do not, we can begin to discern what is true for you and what feels false.

The adaptive self just wants to fit in. It can often act in ways that are inconsistent with our true thoughts and beliefs. If we want to be more authentic, we have to notice and address discrepancies between our beliefs and our actions/ words.

Begin to examine family belief systems since this is where our base belief systems were established during our earliest and most vulnerable years. Think back to early childhood memories; those that can be readily remembered are the ones that shaped us the most. They are easily brought forward because they were the most influential ones. By examining where our behaviors come from, we can learn a lot about our adaptive selves.

Our authentic-self often has a lot of fear, sadness, and anger. Our true selves were hurt, and that's why the adaptive self took over. To embrace your authentic-self, first, you must love yourself and have compassion for others. It takes self-love for our authentic-self to emerge, and holding compassion for others extends that caring and understanding beyond ourselves. Exploring your values and ethics can help bring us closer to our authentic selves. Often if we are very detached from our authentic self, we don't even know what those values are. Be sure and sleuth out your core values using the exercise in lesson 19 if you are unsure of what your personal values are.

If you are feeling conflicted with your adaptive self and its beliefs held or displayed, and the Authentic self, then you can hold a conference of sorts in your mind. Get comfortable, close your eyes and imagine a large table with your perceived versions of your adaptive and authentic-selves. In a respectful manner, allow each side to make its case, then decide which feels more authentic, which one feels right to you. If it is a different action or belief than you observed yourself portraying, have the courage and personal responsibility to begin making changes. It may not happen overnight, but it is certainly a step in the right direction.

I know that change can be scary at first. We all wonder what our family will think, or the boss, or the guys down at the bar. The simple truth is that it's not about them. It is about you. When you begin to discover your authentic-self and align with your core values, start living those values and enacting more authentic beliefs, you will discover that those people in your life that are important, that really love you, for you. They will stick around, often they will be ecstatic about the change that they see in you. They will be attracted to your light, positive attitude. They will respect your courage and perhaps even be inspired to dig deep and explore ideas and beliefs that feel more authentic for them.

For those people that may not appreciate or understand you conveying your authentic-self. Well, those people may just fade away. Those were the folks that prompted you to establish the adaptive version of yourself in the first place. Do not put people like that in charge of your power, do not let them shape you into what they want. There can be no satisfaction in that for either of you.

Take the time to see your adaptive behaviors, be willing to give them up, one at a time and trade them in for one step closer to the expression of your authentic-self. Once you begin this journey, I promise you, your life will begin to unfold in miraculous ways and you will be empowered and delighted to be finally living the life of your dreams.

LESSON #21

Flip That Script

∞

According to the Urban Dictionary, 'Flip the script' is to gain control in a dialogue dominated by another person so that you are now in charge. For our purposes, that dialogue is the one that is going on inside of you.

The stories we tell other people are the stories we tell ourselves. We use these stories to explain who we are, why we are the way we are, and our capabilities. Certainly, these stories that we tell have a function. They help us to understand ourselves and to determine our place in the world around us. Many of our stories about ourselves are based on our beliefs about our abilities and/or the outcomes of certain actions and behaviors.

What if some of these stories that we tell ourselves and consequently tell others about ourselves are not true? What if they are false, but we hold them as personal truths? What if many of the beliefs about ourselves, our talents, our abilities to earn money, our ability to attract or receive love were false? Who would tell themselves things about themselves that aren't factual or accurate?

The answer to the above questions is each and every one of us. We all tell ourselves things that just aren't true or don't need to be. Limiting beliefs are beliefs that hold us back and inhibit our actions and behaviors. We often tell others about these limitations that have been falsely placed on us, either by ourselves or others, typically as a mode of protection.

In researching this topic, I found a great metaphor for limiting beliefs and the power they can hold over us if we stay unaware of their presence and purpose. For nearly 200 years, in medieval Europe between 1500 and 1700, a bizarre limiting belief swept the land known as the 'Glass Delusion.' Essentially people believed that they were made of glass and that they were in danger of shattering into a million pieces if they were struck or run into by another person. This belief impregnated itself in the wealthy as well as the common man, leading to all manner of reactionary behaviors.

We look at this belief now as sheer nonsense; our understanding of the human body and its composition is widespread today. Are we really all that different when it comes to our personal limiting beliefs? Whereas we know that our bodies will not physically shatter, do we not believe that if someone we love rejects us, that we too will in fact shatter, if only internally? Do we view failure or the fear of failure as something that will destroy us? What about the judgement of others for speaking our truth? Does that not leave us broken inside, feeling flawed in some way?

We have all experienced limiting beliefs in our lives, as hard as it is to comprehend that highly functioning beings such as we are, would purposely place limits on ourselves seems logically preposterous, but we do.

Our self limiting beliefs do not just show up one day, they are a culmination of fears, experiences and social programming set in place when we were young. Some self limiting beliefs are passed down from generation to generation, typically by well meaning family members, unaware that they are perpetuating a falsehood. Limiting beliefs can also come from teachers, coaches, clergy, mentors, cultural norms, television, and childhood experiences. Many of them form in the first seven years as we have discussed in earlier lessons, when the brain is developing and we are being programmed to interact with the world around us. Limiting beliefs can be very personal or specific. Here are some examples of limiting beliefs that are common. See if any resonate with you:

I am not worthy (money, love, etc.)

I am not _____ enough (smart, pretty, talented)

I don't deserve it (money, love, success)

I don't have enough (time, money, health)

There isn't enough to go around, so I will do the right thing and miss out

It's not very spiritual to have lots of money

I don't want people to think I am _____

Anyone that is rich must be a crook or a scam artist

I just don't trust myself

I can't handle this

I am going to fail anyway, so why bother trying

Other people's opinion of me are more important than my own

These are very common limiting beliefs; I know that I have experienced many of them myself. This lesson is called 'Flip that Script' because when we are living from these self-limiting beliefs, it is as though we live by a script that someone else has written for us. We do not want to keep living in ways that do not serve our highest good. After all, we are awakening; we are looking to live consciously, with insight and awareness. We are the truth seekers; we do not want to live or conduct ourselves according to falsehoods, not of our choosing.

What we want to do, when we encounter a self-limiting belief, within ourselves, because they are sneaky and have been hiding in plain sight for a long time, is to tell ourselves a different story. One that contradicts the falsehood, we want to rewrite our own script, to replace the one we have been following. Tear out that page and rewrite something new, compose more meaningful lines, words, phrases, and ideas that work FOR us, not against us. Stories and suggestions that highlight opportunities rather than limitations.

I have had many self-limiting beliefs that have been perpetuated throughout my life. Identifying and characterizing the way I lived, acted, and reacted. Though I have learned to 'Flip that Script,' I still find them popping up from time to time. So this is also, like so many other lessons we have discussed, not a one-time fix, but a practice of living. A journey of change and renewal. The more you become aware and practice, the more fluid and natural it will feel.

One of my most pervasive and, at times, crippling self-limiting beliefs is surrounding computers and electronic technology. When I was born, the first wave of home computers was just coming to the market, primitive as they were, at the time, they were considered almost magic. By the 1st and 2nd grade, they were being integrated into the classroom. I thought they were cool like other kids. A friend's family had one we could use. It had games and could do so many different things; even though I didn't really understand them, I had no fear and thought they were awesome.

At the time, my father worked for a large company called Kodak, they were a film company, but were at the leading edge of digital technology with huge research and development projects. I would hear stories about how difficult the transition to these technologies was; my father swore he would never have a computer in his house. He had to look at one all day, no way he wanted one in his house. Other kids had video game systems; we did not need video game systems I was told; they were useless.

As all young children do, I absorbed the disdain towards technology that was being expressed at home. As I progressed in school, the computers became more and more complex each year; I had some fun experiences and some not-so-fun experiences. I got a poor grade on a project in 6th grade because I was unable to properly program code for some machine that was hooked to the computer and was reprimanded for it. On and on it went.

In high school, the computer programming class had accelerated, and only a few students really could keep up; the rest of us basically copied them. Then there were rumors of a worldwide web. When I got to college, they forced us to set up an email account. Most of my friends thought that this new thing was really cool. They would ask me if I got the email they sent me. I would ask them what the message was; they were standing right there, they told me to check my email, they thought it was fun, I didn't see the point.

When I would have to write papers, I would become very frustrated and need lots of help from the lab techs. It was very frustrating for me because you see, I am not good with computers. I had no use for this technology. To me, it was pointless and not something that I enjoyed in my life.

When I graduated college, I didn't touch a computer for a decade until I wanted to open my own business. At this point, my self-limiting belief of "I am not good with computers" had put me so far behind where everyone else was that it was a daunting task to try and catch up. It would be another ten years or so before I would learn about self limiting beliefs. One of the advisors I spoke to at the BPC (Bob Proctor Coaching) program pointed out to me how this belief was not serving me now, nor would it in the future as our ever-expanding world becomes more and more interconnected and dependent on these technologies.

It was suggested to me that I 'Flip that Script' from "I am not good with computers" to "Technology is my friend, it is enjoyable and easy to use these powerful tools for success." This became an affirmation for me. I would write it out as part of my daily gratitude and after only a short while I began experiencing a big difference.

I began to shift into opportunity and possibility as I saw that computers and technology were vitally important. That I was an intelligent individual that could work these devices, even troubleshoot and work through issues, if they arose. If I got frustrated, I would reach out and ask for help, learning along the way, rather than berating myself for not being good enough.

Soon I was helping others set up Zoom accounts and willing to learn more about apps and websites, banking online, etc. —stuff that many people find to be no-brainers. Now with a renewed mindset I am able to join them and make up for lost time. I am by no means a technical guru. I am still reserved about certain things, but when I need to get something done or learn a new task, it is less scary, and I have confidence that I can get it done.

All of this was achieved by nothing more than flipping that script that I had been acting out for so many decades, truly. Finding an opposite message that felt good and served me rather than limiting me. Let's take a few examples of our limiting beliefs and find some alternatives so that we can see how that looks:

Limiting belief: I am not worthy of love.

Flip that Script: All people are worthy of love, myself included.

Sometimes it helps to take the spotlight off of yourself and be more general, this can distance you from the emotional stimuli that has driven you for so long.

Limiting belief- It is not very spiritual to have lots of money

Flip that Script- I am a spiritual being living in an abundant universe; all manor of physical supplies flows to me in vast quantities. Money is a tool and an expression of the good I can offer to others.

In this case, the negative stigma is removed from money, which was the original issue. Being financially secure and abundant makes you more spiritually realized and allows you to use all that money to help others.

Limiting belief- I can't handle this.

Flip that Script- I have always handled every situation that has come into my life to the best of my ability; this is no different. Therefore I can handle anything that comes my way

-or-

Every situation in my life, I know, comes to me to guide me towards my highest good. What is the highest good for me here?

As you can see, there is no one 'right' way to go about it. Whatever feels empowering to you is the best way. When you uncover or catch yourself reciting those old limiting beliefs, write them down, then search your heart for the opposite, a phrase or belief that serves you. Write it out, make it an affirmation or part of your gratitude practice "I am so Happy and Grateful now that (insert serving affirmation)."

I can tell you from personal experience that Flipping that Script can change both your inward and outward attitude towards life. Now you will be writing the script that you are acting out and calling the shots, not some worn-out old behavior pattern that you adopted as a child without your consent, likely from someone else that did not choose it and absent-mindedly passed it to you.

Remember that with self-awareness comes self-responsibility. It is our duty to ourselves and to future generations to make these changes and become more deliberate creators. Imagine a world where we have all flipped that old script and begun actively writing new material for ourselves, empowering material and acting on that. Imagine a wonderful world of possibilities as everyone manifests the life of their dreams. Just imagine.

LESSON #22

Everything is a Win

∽

"Winning doesn't always mean being first,
winning means you're doing better than you have ever done before."
—Bonnie Blair

Like so many of the lessons we have learned so far, this one is about mindset. To be more specific, it is about having a winning mindset. That may leave you with some questions; perhaps you have not envisioned yourself as a winner before. Maybe you, like myself, have always thought of yourself as a bit of a loser.

I was picked last in gym class, not particularly athletic, disinterested in clubs and games where competition was encouraged. I fell into every category, especially in school. But once you get into the real world, the winners and the losers are a bit more difficult to determine.

What is it that makes a winner a winner? First let's define what a winner is, a winner is someone that accepts setbacks and is willing to strive, tweak, adapt and accept temporary failures. It is someone that does not give up and keeps trying until excellence has been achieved. Winners have grit, perseverance, passion and a propensity to move forward despite disappointment.

What we have described is the heart and mind of a winner, someone with a winners mindset. Deep down, we all want to be winners; we all want to win. Win at what you may ask; win at life is the answer.

For our purposes, here, winning is not about competition with other people or circumstances. It is about celebrating all those little achievements that we have been working towards as we have progressed in our personal development. After all, something needs to help keep you going and allow you to express yourself along the way; why not celebrate those wins?

At first, the notion that everything is a win may seem a bit absurd if you have not considered yourself a winner before. If that is the case, then I suggest we start off small; from now on, let's wake up with a win. Every morning, when you wake up, I want you to consider that your first win of the day. After all, look at all of the adversity you overcome just to open your eyes and greet a new day. This past year there were 38,500,000 people that died in their sleep worldwide—feeling like a winner now?

Indeed just waking up and getting another opportunity to experience this beautiful thing called life is a major win, and you haven't even gotten out of bed yet. Once we can wrap our heads around this concept that everything is a win, we begin to see our lives and the pieces that make up those lives in a different light. Coffee with your spouse, a win; again 38.5 million people did not get to do that this year. Breakfast with your children, a win, those moments are fleeting, and they are growing up fast. Did you get a hot shower, win?

More than two million people in the United States alone lack running water and basic indoor plumbing. Feeling like a winner yet? You haven't even left the house. Did you get into your car? A win! There are approximately one billion cars in the world, leaving about 6.5 billion people walking or taking public transportation. On and on throughout your day, you can view these, for most of us, everyday occurrences as wins.

This may seem a bit contrived. I mean, we were talking about winners and what it takes to be a winner, and now just walking down the stairs in the morning is counted as a win. The fact is, 12,000 people per year die from falls downstairs. The point is that we are shifting our mindset to a winners mindset by appreciating the small wins, then we better prepare ourselves and our minds for the bigger wins. Winners exude confidence and expect to win. Viewing our lives as win after win after win helps us to gain and sustain that confidence.

When someone asks you how you are doing, you can look them in the eye and with sincerity say: "Winning." How would you perceive someone like that? As a winner, I imagine. We all expect winners to win. So now, not only do you feel like a winner, you are exuding the confidence of a winner and those people that you encounter throughout your day perceive you as one who wins. That is a win, win, win, no losers there. Soon enough, the term "Loser" will be dropped from your vocabulary.

Each move you make, throughout your day can be perceived as a win. This mindset will fuel and empower you and by association, those around you to meet larger challenges with confidence. Feeling like a winner makes you a winner in the game of life. There is no need for competition because there are no losers. With a winner's mindset, everything is a win, and when everyone wins, that is an even bigger win, well worth celebrating.

Ideas like this spread like wildfire through workplaces and social circles. I encourage you to take the concept to heart. Make it a daily practice to share your wins with friends, family, and coworkers. Start that fire and let it spread where the winds will take it. Imagine a world where everyone wins, each and every one of us manifesting the life of our dreams. What a beautiful world we can create together when everyone wins and every aspect of life is seen as the miraculous occurrence that it truly is.

LESSON #23

From I can't, to I can, to I am!

⚮

*"When you change the way you look at things,
the things you look at change."*
—Wayne Dyer

Have you ever set out to accomplish a monumental task or something new in your life, holding the belief that you couldn't do it? Did you dedicate years of hard work and perseverance, thinking the whole time, I can't do this?

Likely not, and if you have, kudos to you for performing the near impossible. We don't dedicate years of time and sacrifice to things or activities that we don't believe we can achieve. It is only those things that we believe we can achieve that will keep the fire burning inside us through the drenching downpours and gale force winds of life.

Even more powerful than I can, which entails that whatever it is we are seeking to achieve is a possibility is the belief of "I am" which denotes a perception that whatever it is, has already been achieved. A statement of completion. Once a task has been completed, it no longer is a mystery but instead an inevitability. This is the most powerful place from which to manifest the life of your dreams. "I am" is where we all want to be, but if we are stuck at "I can't," how can we make that transition?

First, we must understand what is happening to us. We discussed belief systems in previous lessons; they hold the key to much of what either vexes us in our lives or what appears to unfold seamlessly. Many years ago, I was told by an employer that wealth was a mindset; I felt that he was probably right about that, but I had no idea what he meant, and he didn't seem able to explain it further. He appeared to be operating on some ideas that seemed foreign to me at the time. I actually thought he was a little reckless and crazy with his business, but now I understand more fully what was transpiring, and I am hoping to explain it more thoroughly than he was able with his single statement.

What he was talking about is something called a paradigm. A paradigm has become a buzzword in the past decade or so, but the concept is not a new one; it has been used in academic, scientific, and business settings for many years. A paradigm is a standard perspective or set of ideas. A person's paradigm is their frame of reference, how they see the world based on all the information that they have gathered and beliefs they possess. If we were computer processors, the paradigm would be our operating system. Computers can only function along the lines that they are programmed; they cannot deviate from the parameters of their operating systems. Without a change in our paradigm, we will likely not see a change in our beliefs, behaviors or the outcomes that they produce. When we start to change our paradigm or operating system, then we are looking to shift that perception.

Bob Proctor has a very powerful program focused on this, titled 'The Paradigm Shift.' It is certainly a great way to jumpstart your shift and get you moving in a different direction. When we change our paradigm, we change the way we perceive ourselves and what we believe our capabilities are. We change our perceptions of the world around us and our beliefs about what those interactions mean, in doing so we are able to achieve different results.

The beginning quote is an insightful statement in that when we change the way we look at things, the things we look at do indeed change, that includes ourselves and our abilities, as well as our interactions with the outside world.

I bet at this point you must be thinking, "Okay, that's great, sounds good, yeah, I want to do that. I don't want to be stuck at, I can't, I want to shift to I can, and I am. How can I make that happen?"

To begin the transition of the paradigm we must understand that it was formed by a repetition of habits, thoughts and beliefs. Many thousands of times these habits, thoughts and beliefs have cycled, deeply entrenched themselves in our subconscious minds. This is important information as this is how we are going to shift to a new paradigm that serves us and our highest good, rather than setting false limitations for us. The word that is used to describe the way we will facilitate this shift is called Praxis.

Praxis is a process by which beliefs or lessons become part of our living experience through a repetitive cycle of action-reflection-action. It is a blending of belief with action, over and over again.

The process of shifting is simple on paper, as with so many of our other lessons, there is no quick fix, it's likely not to happen overnight. This is a process that we can start today and develop to perfection throughout our lifetime with each step you take bringing you closer to the life of your dreams.

Start by writing down habits or beliefs you have that are hindering you, working against you or are undesirable to you, because nature abhors a vacuum, you cannot simply cast away these things, as they occupy space in your subconscious mind as well as your life. Instead we must choose new habits of thought and behavior to replace the unwanted ones. It can be helpful to write these things down so that we can be clear in our minds what is not wanted and what new thought or behavior is desired. In order to begin implementing the new changes it can be helpful to write out daily affirmation, remember, the paradigm is formed with repetition, so we must do it everyday until it is a mental or physical habit. Visualization is also a great tool for this process, seeing yourself as if it has already come to fruition can help the process along in leaps and bounds.

Let us use an example that most people can relate to, that was mentioned to me by my previous employer, wealth. I, like so many people, was not raised with a wealth-mindset. Wealthy people were something else, different from us, untouchable, unreachable. Wealthy people were greedy and mean. They had more than they needed, the excess had no purpose other than to show their poor character.

I never even considered that perhaps one day I could have far more money than I actually needed. It seemed an impossibility, so why even fantasize about it. I certainly lived my life stuck in the "I can't" mindset when it came to wealth. My thoughts, beliefs and actions were aligned with, work hard, scrape by, don't expect more than you need or deserve, make the best of it.

Ridiculous, the truth is that I am more than capable of generating wealth in my life. I can breathe, talk, walk, think, make decisions, take action, and certainly use more than I need to survive. Additionally, I am talented, intelligent, creative, hard-working, kind, generous, and willing to do my best at all activities in which I participate. I am sure that you are all those things as well; that's why you are still reading this book, eager for more, looking to be the best version of you that you can be. Come and shift with me.

I would say a person with all those qualities can easily be wealthy in this day and age; after all, there are people out there that lack half of these attributes and have considerable wealth. So, the fact is that I can be wealthy, and so can you. That shift may take some time to really set in, but as it does, you will begin to see the changes, you may start talking about the life you envision for yourself and your family after you have made your first million, that's right, your first million, after all, there are 46.8 million millionaires worldwide and more are created each day, it certainly can be you. Those 46.8 million millionaires own 158.3 trillion dollars, so it stands to reason that they didn't stop at a million. That first million was just a stepping stone.

So now that you are feeling like you can certainly be wealthy, I mean, it is damn near inevitable with those kinds of odds, then we can easily shift into "I am wealthy." We have visualized it, we have created affirmations such as: "I am so happy and grateful now that money comes to me easily and frequently." By saying that, we are planning out our first million and then looking ahead from there.

Now you may be thinking, "but I am not wealthy yet, isn't that a lie?" The truth is, you may not have the cash showing up yet, but that is the result. We are not speaking to the result here; we are looking at the thoughts, beliefs, and actions that lead to the result. The cash is the physical culmination of shifting that all-important paradigm. Instead, focus on those things that you have that make you inherently wealthy.

You have your health; you are alive, that is something that money cannot buy. You have family and loved ones, close friends; those things are priceless. You have a home to sleep in and food to eat, which makes you one of the richest people in the world, statistically. You have the privilege of each new day, witnessing the sunrise and experiencing the most amazing places and things, the beauty of nature, the wind kissing your face, and the abundance of life-giving water literally at your fingertips.

We are all wealthy beyond belief just for waking up each morning, so embrace those things and allow the result to show up when it is ready. It will materialize when you are ready when you have the belief and action structure to support it. Millions have done it, and so can we. Let us celebrate our paradigm shift and usher in a new day as we manifest the life of our dreams.

LESSON #24

No One Will Believe in You Until You Do

❦

"Once we believe in ourselves, we can risk curiosity, wonder,
spontaneous delight or any experience that
reveals the human spirit."
—E.E. Cummings

Throughout our lives we were taught to seek validation from others. We looked to our parents and teachers in our schooling years to let us know if we were on the right track or if we were making the grade. Often in adulthood, we look to our spouse, our employer and our peers to validate our progress or success. Many years ago, my father said to me that he received two report cards each month as a salesman. One was his mileage/expense check and the other was his commission check. That is how he gauged his progress or success. Hearing that left me wondering how I was to gauge those things as I was typically paid by the hour. All I really had to do was show up.

These early validations served us to some degree when we were young and developing as human beings. Now that we are older, does it still work the same? I would argue that no, it does not. Looking to others, especially peers and family, for validation when you are older can actually have a reverse effect. This is because now we are seeking our Authentic selves and growing on a spiritual level. We are looking to experience the life of our dreams and follow the voice inside that is leading us in the direction of our true purpose in this life.

No one else can hear that voice, everyone has a different perspective on what that dream may be and truly the most extraordinary and celebrated people on our planet are ones that go completely against the grain. Ignoring what those around them say, as they follow the beat of their own drum.

How, you might ask, do these people that are following that inner voice, while ignoring the well intentioned advice of those around them, have such confidence?

People around the world that have actively practiced self confidence share the following attributes:

They refuse to be anyone other than themselves
They have a willingness to voice their opinion whether it is a
popular one or not
They have the courage to share their deepest truths,
even if they face ridicule
They have a tenacity and a willingness to keep going when
times get tough
They are comfortable in their own skin, even in the face of adversity

The development of these attributes is usually a lifelong project. Facing adversity and being forced to overcome obstacles builds self-confidence. We can help ourselves by using many of the lessons we have been learning about.

Use visualization to see yourself as the person you want to be, see yourself singing on stage in front of an ecstatic audience.

Affirm yourself each day, stand and face yourself in the mirror, repeat positive affirmations as you look into your own eyes: "I am the most successful salesperson in my field; I am worthy and willing to do whatever it takes to reach my goal."

Do one thing that scares you every day, with every advance in life comes an article of risk; become comfortable with that fact and use it as a litmus test of progress.

Question that inner critic when it arises. I can recall a time when I was young I used to draw these elaborate posters, as I got older and had more responsibilities, I didn't have as much time to dedicate to them. I was convinced by my inner critic that I could no longer participate in this thing I had loved. I deliberately asked my inner critic, "Is it true?" and then waited.

The next day I awakened, inspired to do a smaller drawing, it was very spontaneous and I completed it in eight hours. To date, it is possibly one of the best artworks I have created. Apparently, it was not true. When you question that inner critic, you create the opportunity for a masterpiece.

Set yourself up to win each day, then be sure to acknowledge and celebrate those wins. You will be amazed at the regularity with which they will come.

Help someone else move towards their dream. Often we are at our best when helping others, it allows us to get out of our heads and focus on another. Not only does it make someone else's day and leave them feeling special. It also leaves us with a feeling of accomplishment which leads to self confidence

Love yourself and take care of you. If you need rest, then rest. If you need help, reach out and find it. Do whatever it takes to fill your cup until it runneth over. It is easy to be confident when you feel full and healthy with plenty to share

When you begin to believe in yourself, which may very well be a private practice, done with discretion and care, you will change as a person. Others will notice, it may concern them or frighten them, that they are losing the person that they think they know. This is not your concern. You must care for and nurture yourself in the beginning, much as caring for a newborn baby. You would not just let anyone handle your baby or tell you how it should be raised. Similarly, as you build your confidence by stepping out and following some or all of the suggestions to practice becoming more confident. You must take great care in who knows about it. Do not seek validation from family and peers, it will likely not be there initially.

Once you have gained your strength and can feel your legs firmly under you, where your knees don't knock and your hands no longer tremble. When you can breathe easily talking in front of people and start all those projects that previously seemed impossible when you are actively moving in the direction of the drums— that is when you will have built the self-confidence that you deserve and those around you will have no choice but to believe in you as well. You will be amazed at how quickly they will come around. When you believe in yourself, your abilities, and your judgements, unwaveringly, with confidence, you will exude that confidence, and others will be attracted to it.

They will not remember a time when they didn't believe in you and by then, their support will not matter. Sure, it's a nice bonus, but what you build for yourself, no one can take away. Once you are able to build yourself up, without the need for validation, then you are an unstoppable force, step by step, marching towards manifesting the life of your dreams. I am so proud of you for doing so, not that it matters.

LESSON #25

It's Not Really About The Money

∽

"Happiness is not in the mere possession of money,
it lies in the joy of achievement, in the thrill of creative effort."
—Franklin D Roosevelt

I must admit that when I began my journey of personal development, my first thoughts and perhaps my only thoughts, were how to make more money. As a culture, that is what we all covet, either outwardly or secretly, is to have lots of money. Isn't that the benchmark of success? Isn't that why we plunge ever deeper into debt to 'Keep up with the Joneses?'

Though that was the initial motivation that prompted me to take steps towards personal development, I quickly realized that money was not the only thing of value. In fact, I would say that money is the least valuable of all that one can gain through self education and personal growth.

Of all the books written about money, very few actually speak of money itself. This is because money or the acquisition of money is the result of our thoughts, beliefs and behaviors. The reason that all these factors are far more important than the money itself is that we need to have the proper support structures in place to handle that much responsibility.

Think about it; it is very challenging to run amok on $400 a week. You put some gas in your car, buy a few bags of groceries and pay your phone bill; you have enough left for a case of beer and a few lottery tickets till next Friday. Living this way does take thriftiness and responsibility, but it is very limiting.

In contrast, statistically, 70% of lottery winners end up going broke after just a year or two of receiving a large financial windfall. This of course baffles the rest of us making $400 per week. We believe that our only problem is lack of money, therefore, more money means no problems, right?

Not necessarily. With more money can also come more problems, if you are not equipped to handle that much abundance. It can cause people to throw caution to the wind, spend and live recklessly, without discipline. Receiving large amounts of money without the proper support structure can be very straining on relationships as well. Jealousy, greed, desperation all can rear their ugly heads. The shock of that much money showing up all of a sudden can drive some to madness.

I feel compelled to mention all of this so that we can keep it in perspective as we walk towards the life of our dreams. The money will come when the time is right. It will arrive when we are finally prepared to accept it and to use it in a responsible and beneficial manner. We should all be grateful knowing this is so.

Olympians don't sign up for the olympic games just to get a gold medal, that medal is worthless, just a token to remind us all of their hard work and dedication. Everything else gained through their efforts is what is of true value. Self confidence, mental stamina, physical strength, building a support network of family and coaches, traveling to see new places, competing with like minded peers from all over the globe, these are the things of true value.

Paper money and medals can be rendered valueless with great ease. Possessing all of the attributes of personal development can never be taken from you or devalued like our dollar. Kindness, love, gratitude, excitement and joy in life, appreciation of nature and connectedness to spirit are priceless gifts that we can give ourselves and those around us.

So let's not focus on the money. A Ferrari is cool as hell, but it is not an adequate measure of success and using it to impress someone certainly shows that person is on the wrong track. Many folks living their lives solely focused on money are rich and miserable. It is generally agreed that there are five pillars of true wealth, each of which is important to strike a healthy balance.

Pillar #1: Relational- represented by strong interpersonal relations with family and friends, a sharing of trust, mutual love and openness.

Pillar #2: Mental- represented by an even keel of emotions that serve you on a continuous basis as well as self confidence in your daily life and decision making.

Pillar #3: Physical- represented by a healthy body image and balanced nutritional choices, this includes exercise and outdoor play.

Pillar #4: Spiritual- represented by a feeling of connection and purpose. Faith that all is well and transpiring for your highest good.

Pillar #5: Financial- represented by a healthy return for your efforts, kindness and contribution. The more you give, the more you earn. Waking up every day to follow your passion is never work. Love of what you are spending your time on is a priceless way to live.

In short, it is not really about the money. Personal development, growth, spiritual awakening, they are about discovering the amazing, unique individual that we all are and what we can give to the world. The more you give, the more you get. Remember that we must first give, because that is where the true strength lives. Then we must also be open to receive, with gratitude and responsibility.

We are all wealthy when we discover how talented, loving, caring, kind and compassionate we can truly be in this life. When the money comes as a result of these things, and it will, then be truly grateful for all that you have received and spread the word of what you know. There is more than enough to go around, the pie gets bigger every day. Take a slice for yourself, then give one to your neighbor. Just imagine a world where all 7.7 billion of us thought this way. Now that would truly be manifesting the life of our dreams.

LESSON #26

Be a Risk Taker, Follow Your Heart

∽∾

"Life is either a daring adventure or nothing at all."
—Helen Keller

I would like to start off this lesson by clarifying what we mean by being a risk-taker. It does not mean jumping off a tall cliff without a parachute or driving around without a seatbelt. What we are focusing on here is a calculated risk.

Leaving the dead-end job that you hate and barely pays your bills to focus on the online business of healthcare products is a calculated risk, one that will likely resolve a lifestyle issue and elevate your level of happiness and income.

Making the decision to walk away from the abusive relationship from which you have been longing to be free. Though the process may be painful, stressful, and financially burdened, it is a calculated risk that is sure to bring you new opportunities and healing.

Investing in a friend's fledgling business because you see the potential for success and have a strong yearning to be a part of it; knowing that the potential is there for your investment to vanish or flourish is a calculated risk, one definitely worth taking.

Einstein said, "Nothing happens until something moves." Those words have echoed in my mind for years as a reminder that if I want to see change then I must enact that change, or make room for it to show up. Often we find ourselves stuck in a repetitive cycle that at one point, perhaps many years ago, served a purpose in our lives. Likely it solved a problem from our past but has outgrown its usefulness. Just as a stagnant pond reeks with the stench of decay, so are our lives.

What we desire is a swift-moving current, bringing with it fresh oxygenated water and the smooth, fluid maneuvering of obstacles. A trout in a pond will slowly die of malnourishment and oxygen deprivation though it lives in relative safety. That is no life for a creature that craves speed and excitement, one that possesses the willingness to give its all until its very last breath, swimming against the current, undeterred by obstacles, to reach its destination in the spawning grounds. Sure, it may get eaten by a bear along the way, but those incidents are few and far between.

So are we, in our human lives, either dying a slow suffocating death in relative safety or giving it our all, with determination to reach the promised land. There are so many sayings to illustrate the point of 'nothing ventured, nothing gained' risk-taking. When I was in high school, there were phrases like: "No fear" and "Just do it." Even though these were likely advertising slogans, they nonetheless instilled a feeling of possibility. To release fear of the unknown and embrace faith that your heart knows, what's best is at the forefront of all accomplishments. No one that is a success has tiptoed fearfully forward. Instead, one must go boldly forth.

We have discussed in previous lessons all of the things necessary to have the courage to move forward and follow the yearning in our hearts. We can easily measure what will be given up when we step out and bet on ourselves. What is impossible to measure is what we will gain when we throw all the cards on the table. So let us embrace change, nurture a willingness to take some risks, and follow your heart's desires, whatever they may be. At first it may not make you popular or rich but you will experience a newfound freedom that playing it safe will never produce.

Remember that the song in your heart will always lead you in the direction of your true purpose and your highest good. Follow it, protect it and have faith that you are on the right track. You have what it takes to create the life of your dreams, and when you do, that feeling will radiate out to those around you, effectively raising the consciousness of our planet. That is how important your dreams are, so take the leap, step out and bet on yourself; our world needs your faith and courage. I, for one, am so happy and grateful that you did. Together, we have literally changed our world. We are actively manifesting the life of your dreams.

LESSON #27

Let It Be Easy, Don't Overthink It

∽

"Dear Me, stop overthinking,
you're only creating problems that aren't there."
—Love Me

The above quote is something that I found online; I thought it summed things up perfectly. In fact, I think I will add it to my personal affirmations list; you may want to as well.

One of the best lessons I learned about myself is that I resisted allowing things to be easy or to come easily. I believe that this stems from my childhood programming, where the message received was "I work hard for money" or "That I must earn my keep."

Now, I know that these may not have been the intended messages, but isn't that how subconscious programming works? It is in the background, flying under the radar; it is very likely that my parents were unknowingly conveying messages that they themselves had received. I believe that it is my responsibility to undo some of that limitation programming for myself, my children, my friends, my community, and for you as well.

So here I am, sharing the simple lessons that had the most profound effects on my life. My hope in sharing these lessons is that they resonate with you and help you quiet and reverse those limitations that, after all, don't really exist.

One of those simple lessons was "Let it be easy." Now, that doesn't mean that I sit back, relax and do nothing. On the contrary, letting it be easy tends to fill up my days with more thoughtful activity. Without allowing my inner dialogue to put limitations and restrictions on what I am doing, I am apt to accomplish much more.

When we overthink things, it usually begins with all the thoughts about how it won't work, how long it will take, how we have never done that before, what will so and so think, I will feel stupid if I don't succeed and Phew, am I glad I side stepped all that, just made a sandwich and turned on the TV instead.

Right? Well, letting it be easy is more about relaxing all that brain activity working against you. Instead, just focus on what feels good about whatever it is you are trying to accomplish and stay focused on that.

Heck, that's how I was able to write this book. I got inspired by an idea, I felt good about it and its message, I wrote down my ideas and got started with putting my thoughts on paper. Next thing I knew, I had half the book written and I am excited about bringing all I am able to offer the world.

See how that feels; it feels good; it feels light; it feels free. That is what we are after when we allow it to be easy and not overthink. Rather than the heaviness of, how am I going to write a whole book, who am I to teach people about personal development, what am I going to write about, and who would want to read it anyway?

I had all those thoughts and more, trust me, but I chose to only focus on the ones that felt good and light. I am so grateful that I did and feel blessed to share my experiences with you. All because I let it be easy and followed through with my heart's desire, I have learned so much more than I believed I knew, and I have created an opportunity to share it with all that are interested.

Had I dwelled on the heavy thoughts, I would still be idling at the starting line rather than experiencing all the excitement, determination, learning, research, hard work, and insight that I got from creating this book. Here I am, thundering down the final stretch, and you are right here with me; what a ride. An incredible journey that we both will remember in years to come.

Take it from me; it is worth it a million times over. Just let it be easy, don't overthink. You will thank me; the world will thank you for your contribution as you easily manifest the life of your dreams. I promise.

LESSON #28

Take Action!

❦

"Do you want to know who you are? Don't ask, Act!
Action will delineate and define you."
—Thomas Jefferson

Now that we have learned so much interesting and life changing material, there is really only one thing left to do. Take action!

All the knowledge in the world cannot make up for personal experience. The joy of learning is when you can take what you have been studying and apply it. That is all that is left to be done. Take action. Take small actions if you must, get some momentum going. Take massive action if that suits you better. There is no right or wrong amount of action, it is all about the act of moving forward.

All of the lessons in this book are designed to be learned in a day and mastered over a lifetime. It is in taking action and gaining personal experience that mastery is gained. It is said that it takes 10,000 hours or five years of dedicated focus and action to become a master at something, hence a masters degree typically takes about five years or so.

This is important information but not something to get hung up on. Where will you be in five years is a typical question. The fact is that you will be five years older in five years and it is up to you today. Who will be when you reach that ripe old age of five years older? Will you be the same person, doing the same things, working the same job for the same pay? If you choose to do nothing then likely you will be.

If you begin to take action and implement what you have learned, listening to the song in your heart and steadfastly working towards manifesting the life of your dreams, then you are sure to be a master of yourself on that fateful day. You could also be a master of that instrument that you've decided to play. Or of the business you've been dreaming about; a master of another language. The list goes on.

The fact is that actions you take today, no matter how small or large, will have a ripple effect that will change who you are in years to come. That is inevitable, so be sure that those actions are beneficial to you and those around you. Make sure that when in fact you do become a master, that it is something you are grateful for and will cherish.

I would like to leave you with some words from the late great Dr. Wayne W. Dyer words that have rung in my ears since the first time I ever heard them in the early 2000's. These are the words he wrote to himself as a young man heading out on his first naval voyage, heading out to sea after reading Leo Tolstoy's *The death of Ivan Ilych* he wrote: "don't die, with your music still in you."

One of the most beautiful and powerful sentiments I have ever heard. Please let your music out, the world is waiting, take action (big or small) and begin manifesting the life of your dreams.

LESSON #29

The Universe Loves A Deadline

❧

"I love deadlines.
I love the whooshing sound they make as they go by."
—Douglas Adams

I would like to wrap things up with a little tongue and cheek humor from Douglas Adams, author of the absurd but infinitely thoughtful: *Hitchhiker's Guide to The Galaxy.* The above quote: "I love deadlines. I love the whooshing sound they make as they go by" is one of the most famous quotes about writing and deadlines. Writers are often under pressure to meet publishers deadlines. I imagine it is commonplace to not meet those deadlines.

Any project, whether it be writing, starting a business or throwing a party, requires a deadline; it can be a very helpful tool. It sets a fixed point in time when you can expect whatever it is to be completed or to show up. Great teachers from all walks of life emphasize the need to set a deadline. Napoleon Hill, Bob Proctor, Maxwell Maltz, Jim Carey and countless others recognize the power of setting a deadline.

Jim Carey wrote himself a check for ten million dollars. He wrote a date on that check, effectively setting a deadline. Bob Proctor stresses the importance of setting a deadline for any goal that you set for yourself. He says that if by the day of your deadline your goal has not come to fruition, set another date. Don't lose faith in your goal. Imagine throwing a big party without a date; are you gonna just tell everyone to show up when they feel like it. How can you prepare for that?

It has been my experience that with deadlines, as the date approaches, I will double my efforts to ensure that the deadline can be met. If I am able to finish the project whenever I feel like it, sometimes it never even gets started. There is no sense of urgency in "get it done whenever," which in my mind is so much like: "Procrastinators unite, tomorrow."

More tongue-in-cheek humor, the bottom line is that setting a date in your mind, writing it on the calendar or setting an alert in your phone is crucial to guiding the actions that you are taking and creating a sense of urgency as you near that target. This is how most things are done in the world and it works wonders. So set yourself a deadline in everything that you do, one that feels right to you and hopefully when it makes that whooshing sound as it flies by, you are very near completion of whatever it is you are manifesting and well on your way to living the life of your dreams.

LESSON #30

A Word of Caution

❧

We begin this final lesson with the Peter Parker Principle: 'With great power, comes great responsibility.' These were the final words of Peter Parker's grandfather in the 2002 Movie, Spiderman. Wise words, indeed.

Now, I am not saying at this point that you are a Superhero, but I hope by now you can see that what you, think, feel, say and do can have a huge impact on yourself and the world around you. That, in itself, is a superpower. When it comes to superpowers, the user must have the utmost regard for the damage that those powers bestowed upon them, and the havoc that their misuse or abuse can have on the world.

This book has been about raising awareness, changing our long standing mental, emotional and physical habits to better ourselves and in turn the world around us. The knowledge that you now possess is for you to work on and improve yourself.

It is not to try and change another. Coercion, manipulation, shaming or any associated acts are not superpowers; those are in fact the very things we are looking to counteract with our new found knowledge. I like to reference the X-men, when Charles Xavier started his school for the gifted, the mutants were destructive, unruly, lost souls, shunned from mainstream society.

Like the X-men, we all can be destructive with our gifts until we learn to harness and direct them in a meaningful way. Once we are able to do so, our actions can have a profound effect in problem solving and to aid both ourselves and those closest to us. This is what we need in this day and age. Powerful people, gifted with integrity and the willingness to apply their powers for the good of us all.

I am aware that my examples for this lesson are referenced from comic books that became movies. In reality, these are just metaphors so that we may more easily remember and conceptualize these powerful lessons by comparing them to something familiar.

Before we wrap up this amazing journey, I would like to take a moment to address something that resides within us all, but for some to a greater degree. In my travels and interactions, I tend to encounter highly empathic people.

In recent years, this gift has gained more mainstream awareness but can still cause a lot of havoc in the life of that person if they are unaware of how to properly utilize it, the beautiful, powerful gift that it is, to feel and connect with others on an emotional and energetic level, this can be a lot to handle. I often refer them to Star Trek; most people are at least familiar with the shows and movies as they have been around since the 1960s.

Whenever the Starship Enterprise suspects trouble, whether it be the Klingons or some other unknown entity, the first order given by Captain Kirk, without fail, is "Shields up, Mr. Sulu." This turns on a force field around the ship, like an energetic armor, so they do not sustain any damage from destructive energies. We too can decide to do the same, each day. Perhaps you feel an encounter coming that would usually throw you for a loop.

Just think, "Shields up, Mr. Sulu" and imagine energetic armor surrounding your body, where anything unwanted is deflected harmlessly. As with all the rest of our lessons, this is a lifelong practice of self-mastery, but it can be done. This is a great tool to practice; trust me when I tell you it can help.

Sound Silly? Perhaps. Effective? You bet. Whatever helps you to remember that you possess powerful gifts, knowledge of their appropriate use is a great thing.

I can tell you from experience that we can easily use all that we have learned against ourselves—usually triggered by things outside of us, outside of our immediate control. It is easy to visualize the worst and feel that the world is against us, that all hope is lost, and nothing will ever work out right again. We have all been there, but that does not mean that this is where we should forever reside.

If you happen to find yourself in that place, the best thing to do is stop, consciously breathe and focus your attention elsewhere for the time being. A pet, a loved one, the beauty of nature, and get yourself back on track as soon as possible. Remember, what we think, with strong emotion, we vibrationally bring closer to us; use the knowledge and awareness of this to your highest good and benefit.

> *"Your beliefs become your thoughts,*
> *your thoughts become your words, your words become your actions."*
> —Gandhi

Suppose you find yourself in a prolonged state of suffering, misery, irritation, fear, anger or sadness. It can be very helpful to reach out to a lifeline. A lifeline can be a close friend or mentor, a life coach or someone you trust in your community to listen without judgement. Having a lifeline can help to bring you back to the present moment and put things into perspective for you; the quicker, the better, so you can continue on your true life path.

It is recommended that you set these lifelines up ahead of time so they are available in times of distress. This may sound almost too simple, but many of us think we can handle things ourselves or don't want to burden others with our problems.

Find those people that are willing and able to help in an appropriate manner and have them on your phone, and of course since you have come so far in your personal development, you are then available when they are having a rough day, needing a little encouragement. This is how strong, lasting relationships are built for mutual benefit.

We all must be aware of our thoughts and emotions; they are powerful drivers of our perceptions and beliefs. When used properly and for our benefit, amazing things show up in our lives. The opposite is also true. So be kind to yourself, be kind to others, and enjoy the magnificent ride that life is when you are manifesting the life of your dreams. Thank you.

Rinse and Repeat:

Conclusion

Now that your head is swimming with new information, it is important to practice these concepts on a regular basis while actively shedding old habits and thought patterns. Much like bathing, it feels so good to let go of emotional baggage, scrub away old beliefs that no longer serve us, to come away feeling refreshed and renewed.

This should become a regular cycle in our lives, and though it will never be perfect, it will feel so good as it uplifts you beyond where you may have ever imagined you could be. The fact is, whatever your personal goals are, you will never really be done, so enjoy the journey.

After all, a journey is not just to go from point A to point B. The richness of the journey is always about the self-discovery that occurs as you move towards your goals. As I am sure we have all experienced in the past, once you achieve your goal, you will desire to seek out another challenge—whether that be a new degree, a new hobby, even a new level of health or development. Once you bench press 250lbs, you will shoot for 300lbs, as this is the nature of man.

The purpose for our journey is not in 'the arriving' but in 'the striving' for more and ultimately thriving in this life. To become the best version of ourselves that we are able, and there is no limit to that other than the limitations in our own minds. This book, the very book that was presented to you that you chose over all the others, is your first step to the amazing journey ahead.

I encourage you to enjoy every step along the way, celebrate all the wins, big and small; each holds a hidden chance to fuel and add to your collection of tools along the way. I also encourage you to not stop here; this book is a starting place, not an end-all. There are so many incredible teachers out there, each using their experiences for the betterment of humanity; find the ones that click with you and never look back.

When you discover new ideas and insights that resonate deep within you or when you discover something about yourself that has been holding you back from achieving all that you desire, these are the steps that jumpstart us all to seek growth and hone in on our personal truths.

Revel in this time as it is a flow of unforgettable emotions and often mind-boggling personal change. Embrace it, enjoy it, share it with people you trust, those of us that seek healing, become healers through our desire to transmute pain into healing, darkness into light, and a strong desire, through the process of alchemy to share that with the world.

I will leave you with these words, words that have echoed through time, as they are timeless, from one of the original teachers in history, Lao Tzu: "A journey of 1,000 miles begins with a single step."

You have already taken that step. Keep moving forward and see where the road takes you. I, for one, am so happy and grateful now that you are manifesting the life of your dreams. Thank you and God Bless.

ACKNOWLEDGEMENTS

⌒

First and foremost, I would like to thank my beautiful partner in life, Joni, for believing in me, loving me, and always being by my side through thick and thin on this journey called life.

I want to thank my family: my father Larry Albanese, my mother Gabriella Albanese, and my sister Sarah Albanese for loving and supporting me for the last 44 years, and I have no doubt that will continue for 44 more.

Thank you to my ex-wife Julie Alberlan for being one of my greatest teachers; she taught me to seek strength, healing, and growth, along with a desire to share what I have learned with the world.

A huge shout out to my sons, Henry and Weston Alberlan, for their continuous love and support. The very existence of these beautiful souls in my life has always pushed me to grow into a better version of myself in hopes I will be an inspiring role model.

I want to acknowledge and thank the Proctor Gallagher Institute and The Bob Proctor coaching program for jump-starting my personal development journey. I am also sending as much love and light as humanly possible to Edit Nagy and countless other caring, beautiful people from around the globe for their participation in the mastermind community, Noble Goldman International, for setting a fire in my belly and helping me realize my purpose and potential.

A big thanks to my friends (old and new, near and far) for each and every one of you inspires me to continue reaching out, showing me the variety of life, truth, and love in all its forms. A special thank you to my best friend and creative collaborator of over twenty years for writing the forward straight from his heart.

Thank you to Michael Ballard for giving me an opportunity to participate in *30+1 Resilient stories*, my first published work. Additionally, a huge thank you to Gordon So for not only making *30+1 Resilient Stories* a #1 International bestseller, but also creating an opportunity to repeat the process with another book: *Landed For Success: Untold Stories* with Jey Jeyakanthan, which reached bestseller status with the help of outstanding people from all walks of life.

Last but certainly not least, I would like to thank an absolutely incredible team of ladies, Kelly K. McDermott Chiasson, Samantha Glass, and Linsey Fischer for truly making this all possible, words cannot express the gratitude I feel. Thanks to their encouragement, support, and vision. This journey has now been made possible to share with the world. I am so happy and grateful now that we are all manifesting the life of our dreams. Thank you and God Bless.

AUTHOR BIO

 **Andy Alberlan** lives on his 15-acre country home outside of Rochester, NY, a labor of love for the past seven years. The serenity and quiet help fuel the creative juices of storytelling. Even as a child, he was interested in writing and creating stories, now a two-time International Bestselling Author, A licensed Home Inspector, and a skilled and experienced craftsman.

Andy actively pursues many interests, including woodworking, music, art, and the study of the mind. He has a passion for personal development and a great joy for connecting with others while providing clarity and guidance wherever possible. His core message is that life is a gift and our experiences hold the key to understanding who we are and why we are here. Andy sends out blessings of kindness and success in life to all.

ANDY ALBERIAN

KELLY CHIASSON

INSPIRED FROM THE INSIDEOUT